THE "MAYFLOWER" PILGRIMS

AND THEIR PASTOR

Contender for the Faith: The Life and Times of E. J. Poole Connor, with a Foreword by Dr. D. Martyn Lloyd Jones

THE "MAYFLOWER" PILGRIMS

AND THEIR PASTOR

BY

DAVID G. FOUNTAIN
M.A.

HENRY E. WALTER LTD
WORTHING

085479 520 0

First published 1970

Published by
HENRY E. WALTER LTD.
26 Grafton Road, Worthing
and printed in England
by The Camelot Press Ltd., London and Southampton

Foreword

by

PASTOR WALTER J. CHANTRY

Grace Baptist Church, Carlisle, Pennsylvania, U.S.A.

HISTORY HAS a way of distorting the people whose lives it seeks to record. This it does by being too selective in its choice of facts. Soon a caricature and not a portrait has been drawn.

Many Americans have a deformed picture of the Mayflower Pilgrims. To them, the flock of John Robinson has an elongated love for liberty and a shortened fear of God. The love of liberty has been severely twisted to become the dominant characteristic of their spirit, while their religion is conceived of as an incidental peculiarity of the times in which they lived. Soon the Pilgrim love for liberty blends with the violent acts of modern anarchists and passes for the proud philosophy of those who conceive of their own minds as the ultimate source of direction for belief and action. By now the fear of God has been shaded into the background.

David Fountain's book is a welcome popular account of the earliest New England settlers, for the present volume helps to bring our ancestors back into proper focus. They certainly were not philosophers of freedom, nor rebels against the crown, but humble servants of God. Only when the king contradicted the Scriptures did they find it necessary to obey God rather than man. Plymouth colony was founded by men in eager search of the best way to glorify God, not by selfish creatures seeking their own independence as the greatest end of life. We heartily greet this work as a corrective to popular misconceptions.

There is a second great end served by the writer. History of courageous Christians serves as an encouragement to their spiritual descendants. The modern world still contains pilgrims and strangers closely akin to the little church which sailed from Southampton in 1620. Twentieth-century heirs of the Pilgrim spirit are gathered in small churches, which are as unnoticed or despised as their forebears'. These bands of quiet but godly Christians will take heart as they recall in the following pages the past struggles of like-minded men.

If your heart has thrilled in worship as you have learned the Bible's gospel of sovereign grace, then you will feel like a brother to John Robinson. If you understand that true religion is a matter of experiencing daily grace and walking in daily holiness, you will comprehend the loneliness of the Pilgrims in the midst of many who claimed to be orthodox. If you have been privileged to be part of a Christian church which functions Scripturally in government, worship and fellowship, you will sympathise at the misunderstanding of them by huge church establishments. You will appreciate their willingness to pay any price to maintain that holy society. In short, if you have followed in the footsteps of the Pilgrims, you will feel that the _Mayflower_ story is quite modern.

The church of the Pilgrims was not unique in their time. Nor is the story ended. Thank God that England yet contains some who believe the doctrine of the Puritans and live after their spiritual pattern. Thank God that America yet contains some echoes of the faith they once planted on these shores. May men of their mettle multiply. May Mr. Fountain's book help them to remember their rich heritage.

WALTER CHANTRY

Contents

Acknowledgments

The reproduction of "The Sailing of the *Mayflower* 1620" from Southampton is from a painting by A. Forestier and is the copyright of The Pilgrims, by whose kind permission it is now used.

The reproduction of the drawing on page 57 of the grave of Pastor John Robinson is included by kind permission of the owners of the copyright of the book in which it appears: *The Pilgrim Fathers* (Then and Now Series) by Gill, published by Messrs. Longman, Green & Co.

About the Author:

David Fountain, M.A., has been minister of Spring Road Evangelical Church, Sholing, Southampton, since 1955. He was educated at Dulwich College and St. Peter's College, Oxford, where he studied History. For nine years he was the Secretary of the "Puritan Conference", an annual Conference held at Westminster Chapel, at which papers are given and published, dealing with the writings and lives of Evangelicals in the 17th and 18th centuries. He also has links with the country to which the Pilgrims sailed, and a ministerial friend in the U.S.A. has written the Foreword to this volume. Amidst pastoral responsibilities he has found time to write this brief memorial to the Pilgrims who passed through Southampton 350 years ago.

Introduction

I WISH to dedicate this little volume to the people of Southampton who, I believe, cherish the fact that it was the site from which the Pilgrims first left our shores upon their famous journey to the New World. This fact is largely unknown due to the greater prominence given to Plymouth as the later port of call, and the subsequent naming of Plymouth Rock, Massachusetts, as a memorial. When *Mayflower II* sailed in 1957 it failed to begin its voyage from Southampton. This not only aroused some Sotonians justly, but served to put Southampton further into the background. I have, moreover, often had the experience of discovering that Americans are amazed to hear that the *Mayflower* actually began its journey from Southampton. The picture of the Mayflower Memorial will, I trust, give a concrete evidence of this fact. I trust, further, that I may be able to put the record straight for the benefit of our City. This will explain why I have included the picture of the *Mayflower* leaving Southampton rather than leaving Plymouth.

As a Minister of a Southampton Church very similar in principles and outlook to the Pilgrim Fathers, I have a personal interest in drawing attention to their views. My intention is not to repeat all the details of their wanderings which, doubtless, are being given great attention by various people in various places at this particular time, but to deal with points that have largely been left aside but are, in my opinion, of the greatest importance. I want to show the kind of man John Robinson was and the influence that he had over his people, since this is surely getting to the heart of the whole episode. We need to know his character and his convictions in order to understand the lasting influence he had. He was a remarkable man, not only for the principles he held, but for the reality and fruitfulness of his faith. We live in a day of superficiality. It was his depth of spiritual insight, and the genuine godliness he communicated to his people, that eventually made such an impact on the New World. It is possible to be very familiar with the intricacies of the story but ignorant of the secret springs that set it in motion.

Some ten years ago my Assistant Pastor, the Rev. Thomas Watson, M.A., was the British Agent of an American publishing house. He lived at Weston, overlooking the Southampton Water, and packages of books would come up by ship and be delivered at his door. These books were largely the reprints of Puritan classics and would carry on their covers the imprint of a Puritan as a trade mark. The Pilgrim Fathers were coming back to England! This venture was soon followed by the republishing in England of Puritan works and those of the Puritan tradition. The number of these books sold may now be counted in millions. It was as though the Pilgrims had made their journey back to Southampton, and their message had spread back in the Old World!

I have a copy of the painting by Forestier (as shown on the cover) of the departure of the Pilgrims from Southampton in 1620. It has been in my study for the last twelve years, and I have had it in mind to write something about their journey. I am glad to be able to do this, at last, and I trust it will be a fitting memorial to their great faith.

273 Spring Road,
Sholing,
Southampton.

CHAPTER ONE

The Beginnings of Church Life

IT IS the year 1630. A man in his prime, aged forty-one but looking older than his years, is writing notes. It is the second Governor of the Old Colony at Plymouth, New England, Master William Bradford by name. He has little time to himself amidst the burdens and distractions of office, but what he is writing is of the utmost importance. He has little opportunity to do more than set down "scribbled writings". He does this, and goes on doing it for twenty years! Then at the end, in 1650, seven years before his death, having "peeced up at times of leesure afterwards" his notes, he laid down his pen. He entitled his story "Of Plimoth Plantation", in which he tells in graphic detail the story of the Pilgrims from 1606 to 1647. The manuscript almost reached 270 folio pages. It was a monumental work, without which we would know little of the wonderful story of the Pilgrim Fathers, but with his help we can see clearly all the important events. Bradford was an eye-witness, and is a safe and reliable guide. For this reason we shall quote him frequently, not only to inform, but to give the atmosphere of the occasion.

This valuable work was lost, it was feared irretrievably, as a casualty of the American Revolution, but in 1855 it was rediscovered and provided a source of material second to none for the historian. Many books have been written on this subject on both sides of the Atlantic. The latest, written to celebrate the 350th Anniversary, is *The Pilgrim's Faith*, by Dr. Peter Toon.[1] This was written as a response to interest in the Pilgrims by those in Devon. When I heard of this I obtained a copy of the manuscript in order to avoid needless repetition. Some aspects

[1] Published by "Gospel Communication", 8s., Linkinhorne House, Linkinhorne, Callington, Cornwall.

of the story are developed more thoroughly by Dr. Toon, while I have given considerable attention to John Robinson, the Pastor of the Pilgrim Church at Leyden.

Bradford's Chronicles begin with the year 1607, but we must go further back: 1575 was the year John Robinson was born. He himself never set foot in the New World, but nevertheless made a deeper imprint on that soil than any of the Pilgrims. He was their pastor, and it was largely due to his influence that the Pilgrim Fathers developed their convictions and made their historic voyage.

We know very little about his early life, but written facts will give us some idea of his ability and influence. Testimonies made concerning him and his own writings give us the best insight into the kind of man he was. He first appears as a youth of seventeen, having finished his home studies and about to enter Cambridge University. Opinions vary as to the county of his birth, but Lincolnshire appears most likely. There is also debate about his college, whether Emanuel or Corpus Christi; however, the latter appears to be the one. He came to Cambridge at a very significant period. Puritan clergymen preached at St. Mary's and other churches, to the distaste of the authorities of the University, and were having a powerful influence upon the minds of the undergraduates.

The most distinguished of the Puritans at Cambridge was William Perkins, the public catechist of Corpus Christi, whose duty it was "to read a lecture every Thursday in the term on some useful subject of Divinity". His learning, talent and grasp of systematic theology were exceptional. He also preached at St. Andrew's Church and attracted great numbers of people not only from the University and town but from the surrounding neighbourhood, such was the quality of his faithful, earnest and stirring sermons. John Robinson tells us that his "personal conversion" took place while he was still a member of the Church of England, and it is reasonable to assume that the faithful and zealous labours of Mr. Perkins, under whose ministry he sat, were the means of his spiritual awakening. He held Mr. Perkins in the highest esteem, as his writings bear witness. Furthermore, he used his tutor's "Catechism and Foundation of Religion" to instruct his own people when he was at Leyden, adding an appendix of his own on matters of church government.

When he had completed his studies he went to Norfolk and began the work of the ministry in the neighbourhood of Norwich. He held Puritan views concerning ceremonies and vestments, and as a result omitted or modified them as he thought fit in his services. The ecclesiastical authorities resented this, and he was suspended temporarily. He returned to Norwich and gathered a Puritan congregation out of the City and from the surrounding neighbourhood. Many of them were subject to fines and imprisonment for sitting under his ministry. A contemporary account refers to "the late practice in Norwich, where certain citizens were excommunicated for resorting unto and praying with Mr. Robinson, a man worthily reverenced of all the city for the grace of God in him". He became very attached to his Norwich congregation; he was a true Pastor. This is illustrated by the fact that twenty years later he wrote from Leyden, on behalf of some who were attacked for lay-preaching, a treatise entitled, "The People's Plea for the Exercise of Prophesying".

While at Norwich he was very much exercised in mind concerning his relationship with the Church of England. "I do indeed confess, to the glory of God and my own shame, that a long time before I entered this way [of separation], I took some taste of the truth in it by some treatises published in justification of it, which, the Lord knoweth were as sweet as honey to my mouth and the very principal thing which for the time quenched all further appetite in me, was the over-valuation which I made of the learning and holiness of these and the like persons [the Evangelical Puritans], blushing in myself to have a thought of pressing one hair-breadth before them in this thing, behind whom I knew myself to come so many miles in all other things.

Yea, and even of late times, when I had entered into a more serious consideration of these things, and, according to the measure of grace received, searched the Scriptures whether they were so or not, and by searching found much light of truth, yet was the same so dimmed and overclouded with the contradictions of these men, and others of the like note, that had not the truth been in my heart as a burning fire shut up in my bones, Jeremiah xx. 9, I had never broken those bonds of flesh and blood, wherein I was so straitly tied, but had suffered the light of God to have been put out in mine own unthankful heart by other men's darkness."

Though he was suspended he still hoped to remain with the Establishment, hoping there would be some modification of the rigours of conformity. He looked for an opening in a chaplainship to a public institute or in some private chapel. He applied to the Corporation of Norwich for the Mastership of the Great Hospital, but was disappointed. He became pessimistic as to further reformation in the Established Church and convinced that all attempts at harmonising his scriptural views with canonical law could not be done. He was suspected, informed on and oppressed, and solemnly resolved "on most sound and unresistible convictions" to carry out his puritanical principles to their just consequences, and to separate himself altogether from the church of his youth and his affections.

In 1604 John Robinson resigned the fellowship of his Cambridge College and joined himself formally to the Separatists. This required great faith, since persecution awaited him at every step. The King and the bishops were determined to imprison, fine or banish all dissidents from the Church of England. He went to Lincolnshire, his county, where he found large numbers of Separatist brethren who met for worship as often as they could escape from the eyes of their persecutors. They had previously constituted themselves into a church by a solemn covenant with the Lord and with each other, in the fellowship of the Gospel, "to walk in all His ways made known or to be made known unto them according to their best endeavours whatever it should cost them".

The man who had the greatest influence upon the pilgrims after John Robinson, and who was a leading figure in the Scrooby Separatist Congregation, was William Brewster. He became Robinson's ruling elder at Leyden and accompanied the Pilgrims to the New World. It was in his home at Scrooby that the story of the Pilgrims themselves begins. In 1575 he came to live in the old manor house which was the property of the Archbishop of York but was rented to his family. On that date his father was appointed as overseer of Scrooby Manor for his services in collecting rents and memorial fees, etc. His father was given use of the Manor House and grounds and a nominal salary. Brewster went to Peter House, Cambridge, in December 1580. Just before his arrival Robert Browne, a graduate of Corpus Christi College, had raised a stir with his "forward" Puritan sermons, and was forced to retire to Norwich. He had rejected Calvin's thesis that reform of the Church had to wait for the State to take action. He said that the Kingdom of God "was not to be begun by whole Parishes, but rather by the worthiest, were there ever so few". They should secede in every Parish and form themselves in a separate body under a mutual covenant, "to forsake and deny all ungodliness and wicked fellowships". These ideas were not new but had been spread by the German Annabaptists and Dutch Mennonites whom Browne had known at Norwich. He believed that every congregation should be a voluntary body and not subject to central authority for organisation of any kind. He could see no grounds in Scripture for any such thing. Browne himself later returned to the Church of England, but he had sown seeds in the hearts of many, including that of Brewster. Brewster did not take a degree, but having attained a knowledge of Latin and Greek entered the service of a godly gentleman, Sir William Davidson, one of Elizabeth's Ministers of State. He was an avowed Puritan, who was pleased to converse with him frequently on spiritual things and treat him more like "a son than a servant". He returned to Scrooby in 1589, and soon won the respect of his neighbours, being held "in good esteem among them, especially the godly and religious". He forwarded the Puritan cause at the cost of considerable sacrifice, for he was "commonly deepest in the charge and sometimes above his abilities". He was "of a very cheerful spirit, very sociable and pleasant among his friends", and towards the poor and unfortunate "tender hearted". Only those offended him who "put on airs and a proud spirit when they had nothing to commend them but a few fine clothes and a little riches more than others". He was a very wise and discreet man, and noted for his gentleness. He was fervent and faithful in forwarding the work of the Kingdom. "Doing the best he could and walking according to the light he saw till the Lord revealed further to him."

We know nothing at all about the physical appearance of any of the Pilgrims except Edward Winslow, three times Governor of Plymouth, who had his portrait painted on one occasion. They had little interest in telling us anything about their personal appearance or physical characteristics. Spiritual things counted more with them; they knew that these alone would endure.

Brewster had good fellowship and much in common with Richard Clyfton, Rector of Babworth, six miles away. He was a Puritan preacher who had gained considerable influence and many followers from miles around. They would sit at the feet of "grave and reverend" Mr. Clyfton every Sabbath morning and occasionally during the week William would take his wife and child, Jonathan, with him. In that same company was young William Bradford—perhaps the most able and gifted of the Pilgrim Fathers. By the age of twelve years he was deep in the Scriptures and every Sabbath walked twelve miles from Austerfield to Babworth to enjoy Richard Clyfton for his "illuminating ministry". This was the first step in his "holy, prayerful, watchful walk with God".

His elders soon objected to his course, arguing with him that if he kept up contact with "fantasticall schismatics" he would soon lose everything. In spite of all opposition, however, he went along alone, "nor could the wrath of his uncles, nor the scoff of his neighbours turned upon him as 'one of the Puritans' divert him from his pious inclinations and the goodness of God". He came under the influence of Brewster. Bradford had been orphaned and Brewster virtually adopted him.

Things were bad in the country during the reign of Elizabeth for those of Puritan thinking. When James I came to the throne it was hoped that one coming from Presbyterian Scotland would grant some relief to their condition, but things got worse. It suited James to be an autocrat. He rejected all petitions and requests for religious freedom. "I will make them conform or I will harry them out of the land." There would be less liberty than there had been previously. The issue of new decrees demanded the use of the Common Book of Prayer with full and unreserved acceptance of the 39 Articles, suppression of all private religious meetings and compulsory Communion in the Anglican Church at least three times a year. Consequently, within twelve months, 300 clergymen seceded. It became obvious to them that hope of reforming the Church from within was dead.

In 1606, or thereabouts, the brethren joined themselves "as the Lord's free people into a Church estate". The Rev. John Smythe, who had been long a follower of Browne, joined them at this time. This group gathered at Gainsborough every Sabbath from Lincolnshire, Nottinghamshire and Yorkshire. It divided into two distinct groups for reasons of convenience, the second group meeting at Scrooby. William Brewster was, during these days, "a special stay and help" to the brethren. Every Sabbath the congregation managed to meet secretly at one place or another, and frequently their place of worship, ironically enough, where they held their "unlawful" services, was the Archbishop's palace, the Scrooby Manor House.

Not long after John Robinson arrived on the scene the two respective pastors, Mr. Smythe and Mr. Clyfton, were obliged to remove to Amsterdam. Mr. Robinson remained with Mr. Clyfton's congregation, and became pastor of the church he left. This was the congregation that met at Scrooby in Nottinghamshire. Their frequent place of worship was Mr. Brewster's mansion. We are told "on the Lord's day, with great love he entertained them when they came, making provision for them, to his great charge, and continued to do so while they could stay in England". They numbered between thirty and forty communicants. Though "they generally met at William Brewster's house, on the Lord's day", the stress of persecution sometimes compelled them to move elsewhere to avoid observation and arrest. Bradford says that "they kept their meetings every Sabbath in one place or another, exercising the worship of God among themselves. . . . They could not long continue in any peaceable condition, but were hunted and persecuted on every side." They had been meeting less than a year when they were hunted down. "Some were taken and clapt up in prison, others had their houses beset and watched night and day, and hardly escaped their hands; and the most were fain to fly and leave their houses and habitations and the means of their livelihood." These words of William Bradford are fully borne out and sustained by the records of the Ecclesiastical Court at York, in which we come upon the following entries: "'Office against Gervase Nevyle of Scrowbie, dio: Ebor.' It is stated that the said Gervase was one of the sect of Barrowists, or Brownists, holding and maintaining erroneous opinions and doctrines, and for his schismatical obstinacy an attachment was awarded to William Blanchard, messenger, to apprehend him. On his appearance he refused to take oath and make answer, or to recognise the authority of the archbishop; he, therefore, 'as a very dangerous schismatical Separatist, Brownist, and irreligious subject', was delivered by strait warrant 'to the hands, ward, and safe custody of the Keeper of His Majesty's Castle of York; not permitting him to have any liberty or conference with any without special licence'."

On 15th September, 1607, an attachment was awarded to William Blanchard "to apprehend Richard Jackson and William Brewster, of Scrooby, gentlemen, for Brownism". The daughter born to the Brewsters at this time was named "Fear".

Thus remorselessly hunted down by the legal representatives of Christ's Gospel of love, and seeing little hope of living at peace in their own land, the brethren at last, by joint consent, resolved to cross the sea to Holland, where they heard there was freedom of religion for all men. Others had preceded them. The persecuted brethren in London and their former neighbours and fellow-worshippers at Gainsborough had already found a place of rest at Amsterdam, and the number of exiles for conscience' sake was continually being increased by arrivals from most of the counties of England. In the autumn of 1607 they decided to go over into the Low Countries as best they could. Bradford tells us that they felt the decision to be fateful and momentous. "It was much, and thought remarkable by many that they should leave their native soil and country, their lands and livings, and all their friends and familiar acquaintances, to go into a country they only knew by hearsay, where they would have to learn a new language and get their living they knew not how, and that, too, in a land too often desolated by the miseries of war. It was especially hard for them since they had only been accustomed to a plain country life and the occupation of husbandry, and were entirely unfamiliar with such trade and commerce as that by which the land to which they were going did mainly flourish. But though these things did trouble them, they did not put them off, for they were bent on following God and enjoying His ordinances; they therefore relied on His providence and knew the One they trusted in."

But they faced a dilemma. It was as unlawful to flee from their native land as to remain in it without conforming! Emigration without licence was prohibited by an ancient statute of Richard

II. Ports and harbours would therefore be closed against them, and if they got away at all it would have to be secretly, by bribing the captains of vessels and by paying outrageous fares. They made a number of attempts to get away in separate parties, and were several times betrayed, and both they and their goods intercepted and surprised. Their experiences were most distressing.

Bradford describes two such occasions, and concludes: "Yet I may not omit the fruit that came thereby. For by these so public troubles in so many eminent places [Boston, Hull and Grimsby, where they were seized or imprisoned], their cause became famous, and occasioned many to look into the same, and their godly carriage and Christian behaviour was such as left a deep impression in the minds of many. And though some few shrunk at those first conflicts and sharp beginnings, (albeit was no marvel), yet many more came on with fresh courage, and greatly animated others; and in the end, notwithstanding all these storms of opposition, they all got over at length, some at one time and some at another, and met together again, according to their desire, with no small rejoicing."

The city of Amsterdam was the place they made for at first, and that for obvious reasons. It was a city which had stood for Protestantism, for liberty of speech and thought through that long and desperate struggle with Spain which had ended in the foundation of the Netherlands Republic in 1579, and in the Declaration of Independence on 26th July, 1581. The knights, nobles, and cities of Holland and Zealand had called upon William the Silent to accept entire authority as sovereign and chief of the land, directing him "to maintain the exercise only of the Reformed Evangelical religion, without, however, permitting that enquiries should be made into any man's belief or conscience, or that any injury or hindrance should be offered to any man on account of his religion". Thus Amsterdam became the asylum of liberty, and consequently attracted, from many lands, those who valued their freedom. This led to national prosperity, since the men driven from their own land by the narrow-minded bigotry of their rulers were often the very flower of the nation's life.

As far back as 1593 English Separatists had begun to come to Amsterdam in search of liberty, on the advice of the martyr, John Penry. Bradford recalled the pleasant memories of those days, and describes the church life among them. "Truly," says he, "there were many worthy men; and if you had seen them in their beauty and order, as we have done, you would have been affected thereby. At Amsterdam, before their division and breach, they were about three hundred communicants, and they had for their pastor and teacher those two eminent men before-named, and in our time four grave men for ruling elders, three able and godly men for deacons, and one ancient widow for a deaconess, who did them service many years, though she was sixty years of age when she was chosen. . . . She honoured her place, and was an ornament to the congregation, with a little birchen rod in her hand, and kept little children in great awe from disturbing the congregation. She did frequently visit the sick and weak, especially women, and as there was need, called our maids and young women to watch and do them other helps as their necessity did require; and if they were poor she would gather relief for them of those that were able, or acquaint the deacons; and she was obeyed as a mother in Israel and an officer of Christ."

They settled down in Amsterdam as best they could and "their industry and peaceableness as neighbours secured the good opinion of the residents of their adopted country". But their persecutors were not satisfied. "Measures were taken by the Archbishop and others in England to stir up the suspicions of the Dutch against the exiles, both while in Amsterdam and when at Leyden. British agents were employed in this work, but in vain. They remained undisturbed, and pursued their daily labours with satisfaction and success." However, they were disturbed by quarrels in the Amsterdam church, and after about a year storms gathered, and Robinson and the brethren from Scrooby decided to leave then and start church life afresh at Leyden. Bradford describes the incident: "Mr. Robinson's church having stayed at Amsterdam about a year, seeing Mr. Smith and his company was fallen into contention with the church that was there before him, and that the flames thereof were like to break out in that ancient church itself as afterwards lamentably came to pass, which Mr. Robinson and church prudently foreseeing, they think it best to remove in time before they were any way engaged with the same; though they knew it would be very much to the prejudice of their outward interest, as it proved to be. Yet valuing peace and spiritual comfort above other riches, they therefore remove to Leyden about the beginning of the twelve years' truce between the Dutch and the Spaniards, choose Mr. Brewster assistant to him in the place of an elder, and then live in great love and harmony both among themselves and their neighbouring citizens for above eleven years, till they remove to New England."

Having made this decision, Robinson and his people made formal application to the authorities of Leyden for permission to live in that city. We have a record of this application:

To the Honorable the Burgomasters and Court of the city of Leyden: With due submission and respect, *Jan Robarthse*, minister of the Divine Word, and some of the members of the Christian Reformed Religion, born in the kingdom of Great Britain, to the number of one hundred persons, or thereabouts, men and women, represent that they are desirous of come to live in this city, by the first of May next, and to have the freedom thereof in carrying on their trades, without being a burden in the least to any one. They therefore address themselves to your Honors, humbly praying that your Honors will be pleased to grant them free consent to betake themselves as aforesaid.

Mr. Robinson and his congregation arrived in Leyden in 1609, "a fair and beautiful city, and of a sweet situation, but made more famous by the University wherewith it was adorned. It was a town of great resort in consequence of the celebrity of its University. Genteel families from various parts of the continent and from England settled there for the superior advantages of education it afforded." His first objective was to find a suitable place in which to conduct the public worship, and when these arrangements were completed the church was reorganised. He received a call from their members to become their Pastor, and Mr. Brewster was appointed as his ruling elder. He considered it necessary to be ordained by the whole church. He tells us, "I was ordained publicly upon the solemn call of the church in which I serve, both in respect of the ordainers and the ordained." He constantly insisted in his reference to the subject that ordination was a church act, and for a specific church; it could not be performed scripturally by any other parties called in to officiate on the occasion.

Once settled over his flock he zealously devoted himself to study, and to work on their behalf. He frequently attended lectures at the University and eventually became one of its members. This, later on, even put him beyond the control of the town Magistrates, and gave him various privileges.

CHAPTER TWO

The Congregation at Leyden

JOHN ROBINSON was but thirty-two years of age when he took charge of the flock in Leyden, Holland, but he soon gained an enviable reputation for learning and piety, and great influence by means of it. Even those who were his enemies because of his separation from the Church of England and of the views he expressed for doing so, called him "the most learned, polished and modest spirit that ever separated from the Church of England". His character has been briefly but beautifully drawn by Governor Bradford. "As he was a man learned, and of solid judgment, and of a quick, sharp wit, so was he also of a tender conscience and very sincere in all ways, a hater of hypocrisy and dissimulation, and would be very plain with his best friends. He was very courteous, affable and sociable in his conversation, and towards his own people especially. He was an acute and expert disputant, very quick and ready, and had much bickering with the Arminians, who stood more in fear of him than of any in the University. He was never satisfied with himself till he had searched any cause or argument he had to deal in thoroughly and to the bottom; and we have heard him sometimes say to his familiars that many times, both in writing and disputation, he knew he had sufficiently answered others, but many times not himself; and was ever desirous of any light, and the more able, learned and holy the persons were, the more he desired to confer and reason with them. He was very profitable in his ministry, and comfortable to his people. He was much beloved of them, and as loving was he unto them, and entirely sought their good for soul and body. In a word, he was much esteemed and reverenced of all that knew him, and that were acquainted with his abilities, both of friends and strangers."

He was a man of rare foresight and prudence; and his advice to move to Leyden in order to separate from the strife in the Amsterdam Church before things got out of hand was a wise decision. He plainly saw what would happen as contention in Amsterdam grew. Though a man of peace he knew when to speak and on what side, and was ready to "contend earnestly for the faith once delivered to the saints", though not without thoroughly understanding the matter debated. Bradford describes his abilities "besides his singular abilities in divine things, wherein he excelled, he was able also to give direction in civil affairs, and to foresee danger and inconveniences; by which means he was very helpful to their outward estates; and so was every way as a common father unto them. And none did more offend him than those that were close and cleaving to themselves, and retired from the common good; as also such as would be stiff and rigid in matters of outward order, and inveigh against the evils of others, and yet be remiss in themselves, and not so careful to express a virtuous conversation. They in like manner had ever a reverent regard unto him, and had him in precious estimation, as his worth and wisdom did deserve."

It was not surprising, therefore, that this Pilgrim Church, under the guidance of such a Pastor, should flourish in Leyden during the years it was settled there; years in which they enjoyed "much sweet and delightful society, and spiritual comfort together in the ways of God, under the able ministry and prudent government of Mr. John Robinson and Mr. William Brewster, who was an assistant unto him in the place of an elder, unto which he was now called and chosen by the church, and lived together in peace and love and holiness. And many came unto them from divers parts of England so as they grew a great congregation. And if at any time any difference did arise, or offences broke out, (as it cannot be but that sometimes there will, even among the best of men), they were ever so met with and nipped in the head betimes, or otherwise so well composed, as still love, peace, and communion was continued, or else the church purged of those that were incurable and incorrigible, when, after much patience used, no other means would serve; which seldom comes to pass."

It is not irrelevant for us to consider here Robinson's own view of his relationship to his own people. "This we believe to be a scriptural view of the kind of government which bishops or elders should have in the church: a moral and spiritual rule, which is divested of all worldly authority, and totally unconnected with everything like force. The bond between the minister and people, is the most strait and near bond that may be; and, therefore, not to be entered but with mutual consent. It makes much, both for the provocation of the minister into all diligence and faithfulness; and also for his comforts in all the trials and temptations which befall him in his ministry, when he considereth how the people unto whom he ministereth have committed that rich treasure of their souls, in the Lord, yea, I may say, of their very 'faith' and 'joy' to be helped forward unto salvation—to his care and charge, by their free and voluntary choice of him. It much furthers the love of the people to the person of their minister, and so, consequently, their obedience unto his doctrine and government, when he is such a one as they, in duty unto God and love of their own salvation, have choice; as, on the contrary, it leaves them without excuse, if they either perfidiously forsake or unprofitably use such a man's holy service and ministration."

From time to time, various parties "from divers parts of England" joined the Congregational Church at Leyden, until they became somewhat numerous. The author of the New England Chronology says, "They grew a great congregation." It is probable that they reached two or three hundred. Whatever might be the accessions to the Church, we do not find that they disturb the peace of the community.

While Bradford and the rest of the exiles were occupied in humbler callings, William Brewster, as a Cambridge man and therefore of scholarly tastes, earned his living at first by giving lessons in English to students of the University anxious to acquire the language. We are told that he drew up rules for them "to learn it by, after the Latin manner", so that "many gentlemen, both Danes and Germans, resorted to him, some of them being great men's sons", until "his outward condition was mended, and he lived well and plentifully". Gradually he drifted into other employment more closely linked with the furtherance of the principles for which he and his brethren went into exile. Together with Thomas Brewer he set up a press mainly for the purpose of producing books in defence of their church principles, such as were not allowed to be printed in England. Other books also of a less controversial kind were produced.

While thus occupied in their everyday callings, their Sabbath services and their church meetings for fellowship were the comfort of their pilgrimage. Bradford gives an ideal picture of the relations existing between pastor and people. He says it was hard to judge whether he delighted more in having such a people or they in having such a pastor. The people had ever a reverent regard for him, and though they esteemed him highly while he lived and laboured among them, yet much more after his death they came to realise how much they had lost.

Robinson firmly believed that a Christian church should be composed of Christian men alone, and that being such they were possessed of the indwelling of the Holy Spirit. Having such light, they were, he believed, capable of self-government. No other power, either civil or ecclesiastical, ought to override the exercise of the right on which such sacred duties were made to depend. Holding such views, Robinson regarded the call of God to service as coming to him through the brethren. "I was ordained publicly upon the solemn call of the church in which I serve."

Bradford comments on this period in the life of the church: "I know not but it may be spoken to the honour of God, and without prejudice to any, that such was the true piety, the humble zeal and fervent love of this people towards God and His ways, and the single heartedness and sincere affection one towards another, that they came as near the primitive pattern of the first churches as any other church of these later times have done according to their rank and quality." In his later Dialogues he returns to these earlier memories: "For the church at Leyden they were sometimes not much fewer in number [than the church at Amsterdam] nor inferior in able men, though they had not so many officers as the others; for they had but one ruling elder with their pastor [William Brewster], a man well approved and of great integrity; also they had three able men for deacons. And that which was a crown unto them, they lived together in love and peace all their days without any considerable difference or any disturbance that grew thereby, but such as was easily healed in love; and so they continued until with mutual consent they removed into New England. . . . Many worthy and able men there were among them who lived and died in obscurity in respect of the world, as private Christians, yet were they precious in the eyes of the Lord, and also in the eyes of such as knew them." Robinson himself bears similar testimony. Their former neighbour, Richard Bernard, of Worksop, had published a book, just as they were leaving Scrooby in 1608, entitled *Christian Advertisements and Counsels of Peace*, in which he had condemned popular self-government in the church by Christian men; whereupon in reply John Robinson protested against this "contemptuous upbraiding of God's people with inconstancy, instability, pride, contention and the like evils, and specially this scurrilous and profane spirit, in which you nickname them Symon the Saddler, Tomkin the Tailor, Billy the Bellowsmaker". He was able to deny the charges by referring to his own congregation at Leyden: "I tell you that if ever I saw the beauty of Sion and the glory of the Lord filling His tabernacle, it hath been in the manifestation of the divers graces of God in the church, in that heavenly harmony and comely order wherein by the grace of God we are set and walk, wherein if your eyes had but seen the brethrens' sober and modest carriage one towards another, their humble and willing submission unto their guides in the Lord, their tender compassion towards the weak, their fervent zeal against scandalous offenders and their long-suffering towards all, you would, I am persuaded, change your mind, and be compelled, like Balaam, to take up your parable, and bless where you purposed to curse."

This testimony was borne out by others who may be regarded as impartial witnesses. For example, Edward Winslow, an able and educated young English gentleman from Droitwich, came to Leyden in 1617, and was so struck with the Christian life of this brotherhood that he cast in his lot with them, and not only became a member of the fellowship, but went with them afterwards to New England, his name standing third among those who signed the compact on board the *Mayflower*. Writing a quarter of a century later he says: "I persuade myself never people upon earth lived more lovingly together and parted more sweetly than we the church at Leyden did; parting not rashly in a distracted humour, but upon joint and serious deliberation, often seeking the mind of God by fasting and prayer, whose gracious presence was not only found with us, but His blessing upon us from the time until now."

Among others of their leaders who joined them, as Edward Winslow did, from observing their godliness, were Thomas Brewer, a wealthy Puritan from Kent, John Carver, an early deacon of the church and leader of the first migrating colony, and Robert Cushman, who was associated with Carver in bringing this about.

Their Dutch neighbours also thought highly of these Christians from England who had settled among them. "Though many of them were poor, yet there was none so poor but if they were known to be of that congregation, the Dutch (either bankers or others) would trust them in any reasonable matter when they wanted money. Because they had found by experience how careful they were to keep their word, and saw them so painful and diligent in their callings; yea, they would strive to get their custom, and to employ them above others in their work for their honesty and diligence." The Dutch officials were of the same mind as the Dutch people in their estimate of the strangers. Bradford mentions also that "the magistrates of the city, about the time of their coming away or a little before, in the public place of justice gave this commendable testimony of them in the reproof of the Walloons, who were the French in that city. These English, said they, have lived among us now these twelve years, and yet we never had any suit or accusation come against any of them; but your strifes and quarrels are continual."

We have a description of the regular services each Sunday: "We begin with prayer; afterwards we read one or two chapters of the Bible, give the sense thereof and discuss it. The first speaker then announces a text and preaches on it for about an hour. Then the second speaker talks on the same text for the same length of time and after him the third, fourth and maybe the fifth." The service started at eight o'clock and ended at about twelve noon. In the afternoon there was a similar service from two o'clock until five or six. After this, church business would be dealt with when necessary.

Several of Robinson's *Essays* appear at the end of this volume. They give us some idea of the sermons he preached. When it is remembered that there was no compulsion placed upon the brethren to attend the worship (indeed this was contrary to their ideal of a "voluntary" church) it is obvious that they were appreciative of the services, in spite of their length. Such was their appetite for spiritual meat that, having travelled far to get it, they wanted their fill! Robinson encouraged what was known as "prophesying". In the afternoon, after an opening prayer, Robinson, or Ruling Elder Brewster, chose a text and spoke on it briefly, then threw the meeting open for general discussion. Anyone (except women and children) could speak on the text or pose questions about it.

There was in Robinson a love of peace combined with a discernment and ardent love of the truth. While he was more ready to settle contentions by the meekness and gentleness of heavenly wisdom, rather than by a carnal partiality, whenever he believed the truth to be at stake he did his duty. Arguments about matters that were not vital he left alone, but anything that damaged the Church of God were, to him, of great concern, and, if need be, controversy. So it was that he became engaged in the debate over the doctrine of Arminius in Leyden. This was the centre of the Arminian controversy that was rocking the Protestant world, and Robinson could not escape from it, neither did he desire to. It is helpful to us, in our understanding of him, to consider this episode, since it makes it quite clear that he held the orthodox views of the Church of England as embodied in the 39 Articles, while differing only in matters concerning the nature of the Church. He greatly valued the sound ministry of William Perkins while at Cambridge, and was himself a thorough Puritan in his whole view of the all-pervasive Sovereignty of God. In this he differed from others who left the Church of England, especially those at Amsterdam who favoured Arminius.

Arminius had died in 1609. The Professors of Divinity elected in the University in 1612 were at opposite ends in this conflict. Episcopius was the champion of the Arminians, and Polyander of the Calvinists. The contention had grown so sharp between them that it was the subject of their daily lectures, and their disciples themselves were separated, each hearing only their own side, as is so often the case. John Robinson, however, amidst all his activities, determined, as was his custom, to examine thoroughly both sides, and accordingly went to hear the lectures of both so that he became thoroughly grounded in the entire controversy, and was aware of the arguments on both sides, "and being himself very able, none was fitter to buckle with them, as appeared by sundry disputes, so as he began to be terrible to the Arminians". Polyander, with several of the most eminent preachers in the city, invited him to take up their cause on the great points in question, in a public disputation against Episcopius. The basic issue was the questions Were men saved through the Grace of God alone, or were they (as Arminius said) capable of co-operating with God in their own salvation? Robinson was reluctant to take part in the matter, being young and from another country, though he had been in the city for three years. At length he consented. "And when the time came," says Governor Bradford, "the Lord did so help him to defend the truth and foil his adversary, as he put him to an apparent non-plus in this great and public audience. And the like he did two or three times upon such like occasions; the which, as it has caused many to praise God that the truth had so famous a victory, so it procured him much honour and respect from those learned men, and others which loved the truth."

While at Leyden, and both before and after the settlement of his flock in Plymouth, he published several works, one of the earliest of which was his *Justification of Separation from the Church of England*, in 476 pages quarto, in the year 1610. Bradford tells us of this work, and of the increase of Robinson's church in such a manner that we might guess that the "justification" was in some measure the cause of this growth. He says that about this time and the following years many came to his church at Leyden from different parts of England, so that there grew a great congregation. Robinson grew in reputation and love among all men, and continued his labours with his pen as well as in preaching until his death.

He engaged in controversy with his pen in order to repel attacks made upon him from England by those who condemned his views and actions. His treatise and letters show his wide reading and diligent research. They were full of quotations, not only from the Reformers, but from the Fathers. He wrote earnestly and expressed himself warmly as was the manner of his day.

CHAPTER THREE

The Move to the New World

ROBINSON'S SPHERE of ministry in Leyden was restricted to the people of his charge, so that there was no opportunity for evangelism. This was not only because of the language barrier but because of the attitude of the authorities. They did not mind him preaching to his own people, but would not allow any efforts to win over others to their cause. This limitation was one of the main reasons for their moving away from Holland. Robinson and his ruling elder, Brewster, had a strong desire to spread their principles and enlarge the Kingdom of Christ. They were convinced that the cause they had taken up was the cause of truth and righteousness, and that its extension would be for the good of mankind, so that they wanted more scope for their zeal and energies. Bradford puts it simply: "They had a great hope and inward zeal of laying some good foundation, or at least to make some way thereunto, for the propagating and advancing of the gospel of the Kingdom of Christ in these remote parts of the world, though they should be but as stepping-stones unto others for performing of so great a work." While they were in England they do not appear to have had this missionary vision.

While they were grateful for the tolerance they were shown by the Dutch, they felt a loyal attachment to the British Crown, and valued highly the protection of British laws. The new settlements on the American coasts, planted under British auspices, seemed to them to present a favourable opening for their purposes, and to provide an opportunity to secure a better livelihood than they had at Leyden. They discussed the matter frequently and convened a church meeting to consider the matter carefully. The question of emigration was fully discussed.

The pros and cons were thoroughly considered. At length they decided, after prayer, that they would be prepared to emigrate when and where God in His providence might direct.

It is important for us to note the reasons why they went to the New World. The fact of their going is far better known than the reasons for their removal. It would be safe to say that not one in a thousand would know the actual reasons. They were a relatively small company in a strange land, depending for their liberty and support on the forbearance and kindness of strangers. Their numbers were now gradually diminishing. Less were coming across to them from England since conditions for Separatists were not quite so intolerable. Furthermore, their own men were obliged to enlist in the Army, or become sailors, because of the shortage of work, and thus left their homes and friends. Their own people were inter-marrying and becoming naturalised. Furthermore, the whole company, having no property and generally impoverished, had great difficulty in earning sufficient to maintain themselves and their families. They were distressed by the moral conditions of the people round about, and by their disregard of the Sabbath day. Briefly, they feared for the future of their community. When the Dutch authorities heard of their decision they did not want to lose such a people. So bright was their testimony that the authorities, in order to keep them, offered to provide for their removal to any part of Holland, or to any of their distant colonies. This they said they would do without charge except for a nominal amount for their baggage and livestock. They had evidently endeared themselves to the people who had received them, and adorned the doctrine they professed in a way that was recognised and considered valuable. Various places were proposed as desirable settlements. Guiana, the West Indies, Virginia were each considered. The last was judged the best place if they might be allowed to found a new colony and establish it on their own particular principles.

They first began to think of negotiating with the Virginia

Company, before Sir Edwin Sandys was appointed treasurer of the Company. Some of the brethren objected that if they simply put themselves as ordinary settlers under the Virginia Company, they might as well go back to England, so far as religious freedom was concerned, and take their chance of hardship and imprisonment there. Under a charter granted by King James, conformity to the Church of England was insisted on as a matter of course, but even good churchmen might well wince under the regulations which existed in the colonies. Twice a day, upon the first tolling of the bell, every man and woman had to attend church on pain of losing his or her day's allowance for the first omission, for the second to be whipped, and for the third to be condemned to the galleys for six months. On Sundays the penalty of neglect was even worse. "Every man or woman shall repair in the morning to divine service and sermons, and in the afternoon to divine service and catechisms upon pain for the first fault to lose their provision and allowance for the whole week following; for the second, to lose the said allowance, and also to be whipped; and for the third, to *suffer death*." The clergy of the church were especially protected. Any colonist who should "unworthily demean himself unto any preacher or minister of God's Word" or fail "to hold them in all reverent regard or dutiful entreaty", should be openly whipped three times, and after each whipping should publicly acknowledge his crime. All newcomers were to report themselves on their arrival to the clergyman, to be instructed and catechised. Anyone refusing was to be brought before the governor, who should cause the offender for the first time of refusal to be whipped; for the second time, to be whipped twice and to acknowledge his fault upon the Sabbath day before the congregation; and for the third time to be whipped every day until he made the same acknowledgement and asked forgiveness and went to the minister to be further instructed.

Rather than go to a colony where church arrangements were carried out with something like martial law, the brethren in

Leyden might as well go back to England and take their chance of Newgate, the Gatehouse, or the Fleet.

But was not some other arrangement possible? It was a crisis, and their pastor preached on their responsibilities at such a time and arranged special periods for fasting and prayer. Mr. Carver, one of the deacons, and Mr. Cushman, one of the members of the church, were sent to England as agents of the exiled company to ask permission from the King to settle in some part of Virginia. Various delays took place, and the negotiations were at times frustrated through the unwillingness of the Sovereign and his ecclesiastical advisers to encourage settlers adverse to the English Church. The influence of the Sandys family, under whom Mr. Brewster was formerly a tenant at Scrooby, was of great help at this point. An interesting letter is preserved, written by Mr. Robinson and Mr. Brewster to Sir Edwin Sandys, in answer to one sent by him for further details concerning the proposed emigration. It gives us an insight into their attitude towards the venture.

To Sir Edwin Sandys

Right Worshipful,

Our humble duties remembered, in our own, our messenger's, and our church's name, with all thankful acknowledgement of your singular love, expressing itself, as otherwise, so more especially in your great care and earnest endeavour of our good in this weighty business about Virginia, which the less able we are to requite, we shall think ourselves the more bound to comment in our prayers unto God for recompense, whom as for the present you rightly behold in our endeavours, so shall we not be wanting on our parts, (the same God assisting us,) to return all answerable fruit and respect unto the labour of your love bestowed upon us. We have, with the best speed and consideration withal that we could, set down our requests in writing, subscribed, as you willed, with the hands of the greatest part of our congregation, and have sent the same unto the council by our agent, a deacon of our church, John Carver, unto whom we have also requested a gentleman of our company to adjoin himself to the care and discretion of which two we do refer the prosecuting of the business. Now we persuade ourselves, right worshipful, that we need not to provoke your godly and loving mind to any further or more tender care of us, since you have pleased so far to interest us in yourself, that, under God, above all persons and things in the world we rely upon you, expecting the care of your love, the counsel of your wisdom, and the help and countenance of your authority. Notwithstanding, for your encouragement in the work so far as probabilities may lead, we will not forbear to mention these instances of inducement:—

1. We verily believe and trust the Lord is with us, unto whom and whose service we have given ourselves in many trials, and that he will graciously prosper our endeavours according to the simplicity of our hearts therein.

2. We are well weaned from the delicate milk of our mother country, and inured to the difficulties of a strange, hard land, which yet, in great part, we have by patience overcome.

3. The people are, for the body of them, industrious and frugal, we think we may safely say, as any company of people in the world.

4. We are knit together as a body in a more strict and sacred bond and covenant of the Lord, of the violation whereof we make great conscience and by virtue whereof we do hold ourselves straitly tied to all care of each other's good, and of the whole by every, and so mutual.

5. And lastly, it is not with us as with other men, whom small things can discourage, or small discontentments cause to wish themselves at home again. We know our entertainment in England and Holland. We shall much prejudice both our arts and means by removal; where if we should be driven to return, we should not hope to recover our present helps and comforts, neither indeed look ever to attain the like in any

other place during our lives, which are now drawing towards their period.

These notices we have been bold to tender unto you, which you in your wisdom may also impart to any other our worshipful friends of the council with you, of all whose godly dispositions and loving towards our despised persons we are most glad, and shall not fail by all good means to continue and increase the same. We shall not be further troublesome but do, with the renewed remembrance of our humble duties to your worship and (so far as in modesty we may be bold,) to any other of our well-wishers of the council with you, we take our leaves, committing your persons and counsels to the guidance and protection of the Almighty.

> Your's much bounded in all duty,
> John Robinson
> William Brewster.

Leyden 15th December 1617.

In the providence of God, and in answer to prayer, permission to settle in Virginia, North America, was at last obtained, with an assurance that though no formal or official document was issued, they should not be disturbed on account of their particular religious opinions and practices. The agents returned and reported to the brethren the progress they had made. A day of humiliation, thanksgiving and prayer was agreed on to seek Divine direction in the present position of their affairs. The day was devoutly kept, and Mr. Robinson preached on 1 Samuel xxiii. 3, 4: "And David's men said unto him, Behold, we be afraid here in Judah: how much more then if we come to Keilah against the armies of the Philistines? Then David enquired of the Lord yet again. And the Lord answered him and said, Arise, go down to Keilah; for I will deliver the Philistines into thine hand." We have no record of what was said except two lines from Bradford, which says that Robinson preached "strengthening them against their fears and encouraging them in their resolutions". Clever, in his *Pilgrim Fathers*, says, "It could not but have been one of Mr. Robinson's wisest, most affectionate, most fervent and animating sermons; for he was full of a devout fire himself in this great Pilgrim and Missionary enterprise; he intended to go in person, and his whole heart was bound up in the undertaking. And every step which he and his beloved fellow-disciples of Christ adopted in it was taken in prayer. If ever a church sought God's guidance, they did. With what energy, and beauty, and heavenly-mindedness he would on that occasion, have led his flock by the streams of God's promises, telling them that they should find the same streams in the wilderness, and brooks to drink of by the way, yea, and in the New World to which they were travelling, new and unexpected springs of light, comfort and power."

At the close of the devotional exercises, the church and congregation discussed the question who should go first to the new settlement, and prepare to receive the others; it was, at length, decided "that it was best for one part of the church to go at first, and the other to stay, viz. the youngest and strongest part to go. Secondly, they that went should freely offer themselves. Thirdly, if the major part went, the pastor to go with them, if not the elder only. Fourthly, if the Lord should frown upon our proceedings, then those that went to return, and the brethren that remained still there, to assist and be helpful to them, but if God should be pleased to favour them that went, then they also should endeavour to help over such as were poor and ancient, and willing to come."

The volunteers for the first adventure were in the minority, and as a result Mr. Brewster, the ruling elder and assistant to the pastor, was appointed to take the ministerial oversight of the emigrants, both during the passage and in the colony, till either Mr. Robinson or some pastor from England should arrive.

The property and belongings of such as were about to embark were sold, and the produce, with the contribution of those who remained, was thrown into a common stock from which the expenses of the ship and the voyage were to be paid. A vessel of sixty tons, called the *Speedwell*, was purchased in Holland, in which Mr. Cushman and Mr. Carver, who had negotiated the affairs of the society with the Virginia Company, with Mr. Weston, an English Merchant, sailed for London to finalise arrangements with the Company and with the merchant adventurers who had offered the settlers a loan, on sufficiently hard terms, for seven years, and also to hire another ship for freight to accompany the *Speedwell* across the Atlantic.

When conditions were agreed on between the merchants and the Leyden agents they returned with the two vessels to Delft Haven, the port of Leyden. On their arrival all necessary preparations were made quickly, and on 21st July, 1620, the whole congregation met for humiliation and prayer. Mr. Robinson preached with deep feeling, from Ezra viii. 21, 22: "Then I proclaimed a fast there, at the river Ahava, that we might afflict ourselves before our God, to seek of him a right way for us, and for our little ones, and for all our substance. For I was ashamed to require of the king a band of soldiers and horsemen to help us against the enemy in the way: because we had spoken to the king, saying, The hand of our God is upon all them for good that seek him; but his power and his wrath is against all them that forsake him." He closed his sermon with suitable and wise advice in the following terms, which were preserved by Governor Winslow. "We are now ere long to part asunder, and the Lord knoweth whether ever we should live to see our faces again. But whether the Lord had appointed it or not, he charged us before God and His blessed angels to follow him no further than he followed Christ; and if God should reveal anything to us by any other instrument of his to be as ready to receive it as ever we were to receive any truth by his ministry; for he was very confident the Lord had more truth and light yet to break forth out of His Holy Word. He took occasion also miserably to bewail the state and condition of the reformed churches, who were come to a full-stop in religion, and would go no further than the instruments of their reformation. As, for example, the Lutherans, they could not be drawn to go beyond what Luther saw; for whatsoever part of God's will He had further imparted and revealed to Calvin, they will rather die than embrace it. 'And so also,' saith he, 'you see the Calvinists, they stick where he left them; a misery much to be lamented; for though they were precious shining lights in their times, yet God had not revealed his whole will to them; and were they now living,' saith he, 'they would be as ready and willing to embrace further light, as that they had received.' Here also he put us in mind of our Church covenant, at least that part of it whereby we promise and covenant with God and one with another, to receive whatsoever light or truth shall be made known to us from his written Word; but withal exhorted us to take heed what we received for truth, and well to examine and compare it and weigh it with other scriptures of truth before we receive it. 'For,' saith he, 'it is not possible the Christian world should come so lately out of such thick anti-christian darkness, and that perfection of knowledge should break forth at once.'

"Another thing he commended to us was, that we should use all means to avoid and shake off the name of Brownist, being a mere nick-name and brand, to make religion odious, and the professors of it, to the Christian world. 'And to that end,' saith he, 'I should be glad if some godly minister would go over with you before my coming; for', said he, 'there will be no difference between the unconformable ministers and you, when they come to the practice of the ordinances out of the kingdom.' And so advised us, by all means, to endeavour to close with the godly party of the kingdom of England, and rather to study union than division viz. how near we might possibly, without sin, close with them, than in the least measure to affect division or separation from them. 'And be not loth to take another pastor or teacher,' saith he: 'for that flock that hath two shepherds is not endangered, but secured by it.'"

Mr. Prince, in his Chronicles, has drawn attention to

Robinson's endeavour to take them off from their attachment to himself, that they might be more free to follow the Word of God; indeed such was their attachment to him that some have considered it providential that the separation took place lest they look too much to him and not enough to God. "There was great meaning in the Providence which kept the pastor from embarking with the flock. They might have leaned too much upon him, trusting in an arm of flesh."

After the solemnities of the day were closed, the members of the church who were to remain at Leyden "feasted us that were to go", observes Mr. Winslow, "at our pastor's house, being large; where we refreshed ourselves, after tears, with singing of psalms, making joyful melody in our hearts, as well as with the voice, there being many of the congregation very expert in music, and indeed it was the sweetest melody that ever mine ears heard". At Delft Haven the party was joined by other friends from Leyden who had come by road, and also by some from Amsterdam who wished to share in the farewells. "And there," says Winslow, "they feasted us again."

Winslow touchingly tells us that "after prayer performed by our pastor, when a flood of tears was poured out, they accompanied us to the ship, but were not able to speak one to another for the abundance of sorrow to part". We may well let Bradford also describe the scene for us in his own way. "The next day the wind being fair they went aboard, and their friends with them, when truly doleful was the sight of that sad and mournful parting: to see what sighs and sobs and prayers did sound amongst them, what tears did gush from every eye, and pithy speeches pierced each heart; that sundry of the Dutch strangers that stood on the quay as spectators could not refrain from tears. Yet comfortable and sweet it was to see such lively and true expressions of dear and unfeigned love. But the tide (which stays for no man) calling them away that were thus loath to depart, their reverend pastor falling down on his knees (and they all with him), with watery cheeks commended them, with most fervent prayers, to the Lord and His blessing. And then with mutual embraces and many tears they took their leaves one of another; which proved to be the last leave to many of them." Winslow gives the final touch to this historic scene. As the *Speedwell* left the quay-side those on board fired a parting volley with their muskets, which was followed by the booming sound of shots from three of the ship's cannons, "and so lifting up our hands to each other and our hearts for each other to the Lord our God, we departed, and found His presence with us, in the midst of our manifest straits He carried us through". It was a moving scene and, as the ship was disappearing on the horizon, the hearts of the spectators, both from Leyden and from Amsterdam, were lifted in fervent prayer for the pilgrim voyagers. They retired to their respective homes, filled with the "joy of grief" and blessing God that their companions and friends had found grace to embark on so good and righteous a cause as that of founding a Christian colony in the remote wildernesses of the Atlantic.

The Pilgrims had a good voyage to Southampton, where the *Mayflower* was awaiting them. While completing their preparations they received a letter from their devoted pastor, advising them on their conduct towards each other, and the course they should pursue in a foreign land.

Loving Christian Friends—

I do heartily and in the Lord salute you, as being those with whom I am present in my best affections, and most earnest longings after you though I be constrained for a while to be bodily absent from you. I say constrained God knowing how willingly and much rather than otherwise, I would have borne my part with you in this first brunt, were I not by strong necessity held back for the present. Make account of me, in the meanwhile, as of a man divided in myself with great pain, and as (natural bonds set aside) having my better part with you. And though I doubt not but in your godly wisdom you both foresee, and resolve upon that which concerned your present state and condition, both severally and jointly, yet have I thought it but my duty to add some further spur of provocation to them that run well already; if not because you need it, yet because I owe it in love and duty.

And first as we are daily to renew our repentance with our God, especially for our sins known, and generally for our unknown sins and trespasses so doth the Lord call us in a singular manner, upon occasions of such difficulty and danger as lieth upon you, to a both more narrow search, and careful reformation of our ways in his sight; lest he, calling to remembrance our sins forgotten by us, or unrepented of, take advantage against us, and in judgement leave us for the same to be swallowed up in one danger or other. Whereas, on the contrary, sin being taken away by earnest repentance, and the pardon thereof from the Lord sealed up unto a man's conscience by his Spirit, great shall be his security and peace in all dangers, sweet his comforts in all distresses, with happy deliverance from all evil, whether in life or in death.

Now next after this heavenly peace with God and our own consciences we are carefully to provide for peace with all men, what in us lieth, especially with our associates, and for that end, watchfulness must be had, that we neither at all in ourselves do give, no, nor easily take offence, being given by others. Woe be unto the world for offences, for although it be necessary (considering the malice of Satan and man's corruption) that offences come, yet woe unto that man, or woman either, by whom the offence cometh, saith Christ, Matt. xviii. 7. And if offences in the unseasonable use of things in themselves indifferent be more to be feared than death itself, as the apostle teacheth I Cor. ix. 15, how much more in things simply evil, in which neither honour of God, nor love of man is thought worthy to be regarded! Neither yet is it sufficient that we keep ourselves by the grace of God, from giving offence, except withal we be armed against the taking of them, when they be given by others. For how unperfect and lame is the work of grace in that person who wants charity to cover a multitude of offences, as the Scripture speaks! Neither are you to be exhorted to this grace only upon the common grounds of Christianity, which are, that persons ready to take offence, either want charity to cover offences, or wisdom duly to weigh human frailties, or, lastly are hypocrites, as Christ our Lord teacheth, Matt. vii. 1–5, as indeed, in my own experience few or none have been found which sooner give offence, than such as easily take it: neither have they ever proved sound and profitable members in society, which have nourished this touchy humour. But, besides these, there are divers motives provoking you, above others, to great care and conscience this way. As first, you are many of you strangers, as to the persons, so to the infirmities one of another, and so stand in need of more watchfulness this way; lest, when such things fall out in men and women as you suspected not, you be inordinately affected with them; which doth require at your hands much wisdom and charity, for the covering and preventing of incident offences that way. And lastly your intended course of civil community will minister continual occasion of offence, and will be as fuel for that fire, except you diligently quench it with brotherly forbearance. And if taking of offence causelessly or easily at men's doings be so carefully to be avoided, how much more heed is to be taken, that we take not offence at God himself; which yet we certainly do, so oft as we do murmur at his providences in our crosses, nor bearing patiently such afflictions as wherewith he pleaseth to visit us. Store we up therefore patience against the evil day; without which we take offence at the Lord himself in His holy and just works.

A fourth thing there is carefully to be provided for to wit, that with your common employments you join common affections, truly bent upon the general good; avoiding, as a deadly plague of your both common and special comfort, all retiredness of mind for improper advantage, and all singularly affected any manner of way. Let every man repress himself, and the whole body in each person, as so many rebels against the common good, all private respects of men's selves not sorting with the general conveniency. And as men are careful not to have a new house shaken with any violence, before it be well settled, and the parts firmly knit, so be you, I beseech you, brethren, much more careful that the house of God, which you are, and are to be, be not shaken with unnecessary novelties, or other oppositions at the first settling thereof.

Lastly whereas you are to become a body politic, using amongst yourselves civil government, and are not furnished with any persons of special eminency above the rest to be chosen by you into office of Government, let your wisdom and godliness appear not only in choosing such persons as do entirely love, and will diligently promote the common good, but also in yielding unto them all due honour and obedience in their lawful administrations, not beholding in them the ordinances of their persons but God's ordinances for your good; nor being like the foolish multitude, who more honour the gay coat than either the virtuous mind of the man, or the glorious ordinance of the Lord. But you know better things, and that the image of the Lord's power and authority, which the magistrates beareth, is honourable in how mean persons soever. And this duty you both may the more willingly and ought the more conscionably to perform, because you are at least for the present, to have only them for your ordinary governors which yourselves shall make choice of for that work.

Sundry other things of importance I could put you in mind of, and of those before mentioned in more words. But I will not so far wrong your godly minds as to think you heedless of these things; there being also divers among you so well able to admonish both themselves and others of what concerneth them. These few things, therefore, and the same in few words, I do earnestly commend unto your care and conscience, joining therewith my daily incessant prayers unto the Lord, that He who hath made the heavens and the earth, the sea and all rivers of waters, and whose providence is over all His works, especially over all His dear children for good, would so guide and guard you in your ways, as inwardly by His Spirit, so outwardly by the hand of His power, as that both you and we also, for and with you, may have after matter of praising His name all the days of your and our lives. Fare you well, in Him in whom you trust, and in whom I rest.

An unfeigned well-wisher of your happy success in this hopeful voyage,

John Robinson.

This letter is not dated, but appears to have been written between the period of the embarkation at Delft Haven and their sailing from Southampton. In the following letter to Mr. Carver, dated 27th July, 1620, reference is made to the letter addressed to the whole company.

My dear brother—

I received, inclosed, your last letter and note of information which I shall carefully keep and make use of, as there shall be occasion. I have a true feeling of your perplexity of mind, and toil of body; but I hope that you, having always been able so plentifully to administer comfort unto others in their trials, are so well furnished for yourself, as that far greater difficulties than you have yet undergone (though I conceive them to be great enough) cannot oppress you, though they press you. Now, what shall I say, or write unto you and your good wife, my loving sister? Even only this I desire, and always shall mercy and blessing unto you from the Lord, as unto my own soul; and assure yourself that my heart is with you, and that I will not delay my bodily coming at the first opportunity. I have written a large letter to the whole, and am sorry I shall not rather speak than write to them, and the more, considering the want of a preacher, which I shall also make some spur to my hastening towards you. I do ever commend my best affection unto you, which if I thought you made any doubt of, I would express in more and the same more ample and full words. And the Lord, in whom you trust, and whom you serve, ever in this business and journey, guide you with His hand, protect you with His wing, and show you and us His salvation in the end, and bring us in the meanwhile together in the place desired (if such be His good will), for Christ's sake, Amen.

Your's

John Robinson.

There was a delay at Southampton because the *Speedwell* had already showed signs of unseaworthiness and had to be repaired. This delay and further expense only added to the burdens already carried by the Pilgrims. As a result of this delay a local man, John Alden, a cooper of Southampton, joined the party. He did not share the Pilgrims' convictions, nor for that matter did most of the emigrants. Only 41 of the 102 passengers were Pilgrims. The others were not concerned about religious freedom but simply wanted a better life in a new land. "All things now being ready… the company was called together . . . which being done they set sail on the fifth of August," so wrote Governor Bradford. Owing to a change in the calendar 5th August corresponds to 15th August, the date on the Mayflower Memorial at Southampton. This change has been overlooked by many, but accounts for the apparent discrepancy.

The difficulties they had met with had been enough to discourage any man from the enterprise. They had been at the mercy of unscrupulous men and had even had to part with some of their necessary provisions to pay bills. But worse was to come. As the coast of England faded on the horizon they felt that they had left those shores for good. However, Master Reynolds, the Captain of the *Speedwell*, did not intend to make the journey at all. He and his men had tricked the Pilgrims by putting into the ship a mainmast too high and with too many sails. This resulted in the seams opening and leaks being sprung. When a proper mast was put in the ship was perfectly seaworthy. Consequently, both ships had to put into Plymouth and, as is well known, the *Speedwell* was abandoned. It was, therefore, due only to the action of Reynolds and his crew that Plymouth ever saw the *Mayflower*! Finally, they left Plymouth on 6th September.

The trials on board ship were worse than those on land. Master Christopher Martin was made Governor of the passengers on the *Mayflower*. He was given responsibilities by the merchant adventurers and had no love for the Pilgrims' principles. It is doubtful even if he had any of his own. This made life grim on the little ship. Everyone was furious with Christopher Martin— the sailors for his "ignorante bouldness" in interfering in things he knew nothing about, some being so enraged at him that they openly threatened to "mischeefe him". Nor did he get on any better with the Pilgrims, whom he insulted and offended, treating them with great "scorne and contempte, as if they were not good enough to wipe his shoes", complained one of the Pilgrims who had been Governor on the *Speedwell*. "It would break your heart to see his dealing and the mourning of our people. . . . They complain to me, and alas! I can doe nothing for them; if I speak to him, he flies in my face as mutinous, and saith no complaints shall be heard or received by himself, and says they are froward and waspish, discontented people, and I do ill to hear them. . . . Where is the meek and humble spirite of Moses? and of Nehemiah who re-edified the walls of Jerusalem and the state of Israel? Is not the sound of Rehoboam's braggs daily heard amongst us? . . . Friend, if ever we make a plantation, God works a miracle especially considering how scant we shall be of victualls, and most of all ununited amongst ourselves, and devoid of good tutors and regimente. Violence will break all."

"If I should write to you of all things which promiscuously forerun our ruine," he told a friend, "I should overcharge my weak head and greive your tender hart; only this, I pray you, prepare for evil tidings of us every day. . . . I see not in reason how we shall escape even the gasping of hunger-starved persons; but God can do much, and His will be done."

They were sixty-three days on the waves before the *Mayflower* as much as sighted land. September passed wearily and they reached mid-Atlantic, making steady headway with a fresh breeze under fair skies. Then, suddenly, the weather changed as fierce storms came from the west. For days it was impossible to carry the sail, and the ship drifted under the bare masts, with a helmsman trying desperately to hold her into the wind. The pounding of the waves opened seams in the deck, letting in icy water upon the crowded passengers. One of the passengers, John Howland, could not bear the stuffiness in the hold any longer, and came on deck one day. He was immediately swept overboard, but he managed to hold on to the topsail halyard which hung over the side and, "though he was sundrie fadoms in water", he was pulled in with a boat hook. He was "something ill with it yet he lived many years after and became a profitable member both in church and commone wealthe". The storm increased in fury and a main beam amidships cracked. Even the captain was alarmed. Providentially, someone had brought along a "great iron scrue", which was used to force the great beam back into place. The sailors were greatly distressed and among the officers there was "great distraction and difference of opinion about whether they should return". Finally, they decided to continue, "so they committed themselves to the will of God and resolved to proceed". In November the only death occurred. It was striking that only one person should die, since ships bound for Virginia at this time often lost up to half their number, and usually at least a third. But most striking of all is the comment of Bradford on the death of young William Butten. "There was a proud and very profane young man, one of the sea-men, of a lusty, able body, which made him the more haughty; he would alway be contemning the poor people in their sickness and cursing them daily with grievous execrations; and did not let to tell them that he hoped to help cast half of them overboard before they came to their journey's end, and to make merry with what they had; and if he were by any gently reproved, he would curse and swear most bitterly. But it pleased God before they came half seas over, to smite this young man with a grievous disease, of which he died in a desperate manner, and so was himself the first that was thrown overboard. Thus his curses light on his own head, and it was an astonishment to all his fellows for they noted it to be the just hand of God upon him."

The Pilgrims had intended to settle near the mouth of the Hudson River, but the tempest had carried them well off course. The first sight of land was the desolate Cape Cod, and there they dropped anchor. Before anyone left the ship a meeting was held and the famous "Mayflower Compact" was signed. This gave every man an equal voice in the making of laws. All the heads of the families, forty-one in number, set down their names, and John Carver was chosen the first Governor. They had to find a place to settle, and for a month they sailed up and down looking for a good harbour. Some of them went ashore several times to explore the country, but found it to be barren. Winter came more quickly than they had expected. Snow and ice often covered the clothing of the explorers. Providentially, on one occasion they found Indian corn buried under the snow; on another they were attacked by the Indians, but escaped to the ship. At last, a safe haven was found on the west side of Plymouth Bay. In spite of the ice-bound shores, dense forests and snow, this un-explored wilderness was, for them, a haven. They decided to land, and spent the last day in solemn worship and thanksgiving to God. On 22nd December they landed on Plymouth Rock. The sea-weary passengers came ashore bringing all their belongings with them. They faced tempest, sleet, snow, hunger, cold and exposure. They had first to build houses, but soon sickness struck their enfeebled bodies. At one time only seven men were able to work on the sheds which they built to protect themselves. Every second day a grave had to be dug in the frozen ground. So many were sick that those who were well were scarcely enough to care for them. If spring had not come early the colony could have perished entirely, but as it was, half of the settlers were dead and many of the children had become orphans. Their sufferings could not be described, but their faith remained firm, and with the arrival of spring they praised God. "Above all, there was freedom to worship God, that dearest of blessings. Only half of our company died. The rest were getting well. God was nearer to us than he ever had been in dear old England. He had planted His vine in the wilderness, and the vine of His planting would grow. What more could we ask." For the Pilgrims it was victory at last. They had come through the long winter through God's grace. The first mild day was 3rd March. The houses had been built, their corn began to grow, but before it ripened they still suffered. Very little food was available. They caught fish, dug clams, snared rabbits, but sometimes had very little to eat. Often they knew not at night "where to have a bit in the morning". Children cried for bread, strong men grew faint for want of food. Five kernels of parched corn were all that a boy sometimes had for his dinner, besides an oyster or a crab. But they survived and many more came across from England, and the Pilgrim Church from Holland eventually joined them, though Robinson never saw them again. It is a testimony to their faith not only that they survived, but that they did not murmur against God in His dealings with them. Their very extremities demonstrated their trust in Him, and calm submission to His wisdom. The first year shows us qualities in their lives that might never have been known had they not suffered as they did.

When eventually they had their first harvest the survival of the colony was assured. It was an occasion of great thanksgiving to God. The 26th November is a public holiday in the United States, and is called "Thanksgiving Day". Thus the faith of the Pilgrims has been remembered to this day in the life of the nation.

CHAPTER FOUR

Hands across the sea

WE CONCLUDE the story by returning to Leyden where John Robinson and the congregation that remained prayed and awaited news of the colony. With the return of the *Mayflower* to England the following year, news of the safe arrival and settlement of the Pilgrim Fathers was sent to Mr. Robinson, and was received by all with deep gratitude. The pastoral relation continuing unbroken, though oceans rolled between, he was anxious for both their temporal and spiritual welfare. He sympathised with their difficulties and gave thanks for their success. Learning that, as a result of the difficulties of climate and hardships of many kinds, many of them had died during the winter, he immediately wrote the following letter to encourage them:

Much loved Brethren,

Neither the distance of place, nor distinction of body, can at all either dissolve or weaken that bond of true Christian affection in which the Lord by his Spirit hath tied us together. My continual prayers are to the Lord for you; my most earnest desire is unto you; from whom I will not longer keep (if God will) than means can be provided to bring with me the wives and children of divers of you and the rest of your brethren, whom I could not leave behind me without great injury both to you and them, and offence to God, and all men. The death of so many, our dear friends and brethren, oh! how grievous hath it been to you to bear, and to us to take knowledge of; which, if it could be mended with lamenting, could not sufficiently be bewailed; but we must go unto them, and they shall not return to us. And how many, even of us God hath taken away here, and in England, since your departure, you may elsewhere take knowledge. But the same God has tempered judgment with mercy, as otherwise, so in sparing the rest especially those by whose godly and wise government you may be, and (I know) are so much helped. In a battle it is not looked for but that divers should die; it is thought well for a side if it get the victory, though with the loss of divers, if not too many, or too great. God, I hope, hath given you the victory, after many difficulties, for yourselves and others; though I doubt not but many do and will remain for you and us all to strive with.

Brethren I hope I need not to exhort you to obedience unto those whom God hath set over you in church and commonwealth, and to the Lord in them. It is a Christian's honour to give honour according to men's places; and his liberty, to serve God in faith, and his brethren in love orderly and with a willing and free heart. God forbid! I should need to exhort you to peace which is the bond of perfection, and by which all good is tied together and without which it is scattered. Have peace with God first, by faith in his promises, good conscience kept in all things, and oft renewed by repentance; and so, one with another for his sake, who is though three, one; and for Christ's sake, who is one, and as you are called by one Spirit to one hope. And the God of peace and grace and all goodness be with you, in all the fruits thereof plenteously upon your heads now, and for ever. All your brethren here remember you with great love; a general token whereof they have sent you.

> Your's ever in the Lord
> John Robinson.

Leyden, Holland, June 30th ANNO 1621.

His letters to the Colony were very precious to the Pilgrims, as of an absent father to his flock, full of wise counsel and the feelings of his heart. He always looked upon them as his people, and they looked to him as their pastor; for to the day of his death neither he nor they had abandoned the hope of being again united. "If either prayers, tears, or means would have saved his life," said Roger White in his letter to Governor Bradford, "he had not gone hence. But having faithfully finished his work, which the Lord had appointed him here to perform, he now rests with the Lord in eternal happiness; we wanting him and the Church governors, not having one at present that is a governing officer among us." Their leading men had gone over to Plymouth, and before many years almost the whole remaining portion of the Church were gathered there through the great kindness of their brethren. According to Cheever, in his *Pilgrim Fathers*, "Never was there a Church, whose members manifested more truly one toward another the patience and brotherly love of the Gospel. This was a great proof of the faithfully apostolic character of their beloved pastor's ministry."

Robinson's spirit was evidently saddened after the departure of the Pilgrims, whom he longed to follow. He remained with the remnant of his church at Leyden, hoping that he, with his family and others, might soon join the others on the western shores of the Atlantic. He resolved, however, not to leave till the wives and children of the brethren who had gone already could accompany him. In the same spirit of benevolence and self-denial which had prompted him to remain on the banks of the Humber with the wives and children of the fugitives, he continued at Leyden to support and watch over the more helpless and dependent part of his Christian family.

A letter was sent by Mr. Robinson to his close friend, Mr. Brewster, two years after the Pilgrims had left Europe, which expresses his earnest desire to embark, but showed the difficulties of his position, and the improbability of a speedy settlement in Plymouth. "Hoping against hope", he earnestly desired to exercise his pastoral function for a few years among his Trans-atlantic friends; but the great Head of the Church was pleased to arrange otherwise, and to call him away from the scenes of toil and suffering on earth to the rest and blessedness of heaven. He laboured in his spiritual and ministerial vocation for five years after the colonisation of part of his church. He was taken ill on Saturday, 22nd February, 1625, but preached twice on the following day. An "inward ague" consumed him. His strength gradually failed, and after eight days he was dead—the first day of March, 1625. He died in the prime and vigour of his days, being only fifty years old. No record of his dying experience or sayings is preserved, but he retained the full possession of his faculties. He was visited constantly by members of his church who prayed earnestly that he might be spared. But his testimony was concluded and his work was done. The foundations of a growing church were soundly laid on distant shores by those "spiritual heroes" whom he had trained in learning and piety. He was no longer needed. The Pilgrims were not to trust in a man, but to look only to Him whose pillar of cloud and of fire had hitherto conducted them, and by whose presence and blessing alone they could prosper.

Mr. Robinson was taken home amidst the tears of his family and friends. Winslow says that such was the respect in which Mr. Robinson was held by the citizens that "when God took him away from them and us by death, the University and ministers of the city accompanied him to his grave with all their accustomed solemnities, bewailing the great loss, that not only that particular church had, whereof he was pastor, but some of the chief of them sadly affirmed that all the churches of Christ sustained a loss by the death of that worthy instrument of the Gospel". Mr. Prince also says that he was informed, when at Leyden, "that he was had in high esteem both by the city and University, for his learning, piety, moderation and excellent accomplishments; the magistrates, ministers, scholars and most of the gentry mourned his death as a public loss, and followed him to the grave".

Bradford held him in the highest esteem. "Yea, such was the mutual love and reciprocal respect that this worthy man had to his flock and his flock to him, that it might be said of them, as it was once said of that famous emperor, Marcus Aurelius, and the people of Rome, that it was hard to judge whether he delighted more in having such a people, or they in having such a pastor. His love was great towards them, and his care was always bent for their best good, both for soul and body . . ." Although they

IN MEMORY OF
JOHN ROBINSON
PASTOR OF THE ENGLISH CHURCH IN LEYDEN
1609   1625
HIS BROADLY TOLERANT MIND
GUIDED AND DEVELOPED THE RELIGIOUS LIFE OF

THE PILGRIMS OF THE MAYFLOWER

OF HIM THESE WALLS ENSHRINE ALL THAT WAS MORTAL
HIS UNDYING SPIRIT
STILL DOMINATES THE CONSCIENCES OF A MIGHTY NATION
IN THE LAND BEYOND THE SEAS

THIS TABLET WAS ERECTED BY THE GENERAL SOCIETY OF MAYFLOWER
DESCENDANTS IN THE UNITED STATES OF AMERICA   A.D.1928

The memorial to John Robinson

"esteemed him highly whilst he lived and laboured among them, yet much more after his death, when they came to feel the want of his help, and saw by woeful experience, what a treasure they had lost to the grief of their hearts and wounding of their souls; yea, such a loss as they saw could not be repaired."

It is fitting to end the story with a testimony to Robinson's God-given faith which was the mainspring and cause of the whole enterprise. He was convinced of the truth of his principles, and he desired their extension through the world. He uttered his belief of their ultimate triumph, in these remarkable words: "Religion is not always sown and reaped in one age. One soweth and another reapeth. The many that are already gathered, by the mercy of God, unto the kingdom of his Son Jesus, and the nearness of many more through the whole land, for the regions are 'white unto harvest' do promise, within less than a hundred years, if our sins and their sins make not us and them unworthy of his mercy, a very plenteous harvest."

The prediction was verified; one hundred years passed, and the great principles Mr. Robinson contended for had spread throughout England, and a considerable portion of America. His faith was given to him by his Maker and Saviour, Jesus Christ, and his hopes were fulfilled beyond all he could ask or think.

CHAPTER FIVE

Principles and Convictions

THE STORY of the Pilgrim Fathers is one that cannot be fully understood without a clear knowledge and appreciation of the principles for which they stood. Accounts which have been accurate but which would not indeed satisfy the Pilgrims themselves as expressing their mind and heart have been written of their journeyings and of their convictions. One really needs to be both an historian and a theologian at the same time to grasp properly what it was all about. In the *Chronicles of the Pilgrim Fathers* (Everyman's Library Edition) we read in the Introduction, "They held (in opposition to the Church) that the priesthood is not a distinct order, but an office temporarily conferred by the vote of the congregation." The truth of the matter is that they did not consider there *was* any such thing as the Priesthood in the New Testament as there was in the Old, but rather that all Christians were Priests who offered up *spiritual* sacrifices to God. They would never dream of calling their Minister a Priest, but rather a Pastor. To many the distinction would appear pedantic, but it is of the greatest theological importance.

Others have misinterpreted the motives of the Pilgrim Fathers by putting down their difference to an objection to ceremonies and little more. *The Pilgrim Fathers*, by W. J. C. Gill (Then and There Series) takes the reason for their decision to leave England as a matter of their rejection of ceremonies in worship, and the belief in the autonomy of the local church.

John Robinson had the same problem in dealing with those who did not understand their reasons for their separation as some do these days who want to tell the story. Bishop Hall, the Rector of Halstead in Essex, addressed a letter to "Mr. Smith and Mr. Rob. Ringleaders of the late separation of Amsterdam" (the designation, of course, referred to Mr. Smyth and Mr. Robinson).

Robinson answers him: "Master Hall, If you have taken but the least knowledge of the grounds in our judgment and practice, how dare you both abuse us and the reader as if the only or chief grounds of our separation were your popish ceremonies? but if you go only by guess, having never so much as read over our treatise, published in our defence, and yet stick not to pass this your censorious doom, both upon us and it; I leave it to the reader to judge whether you have been more lavish of your censure or credit!" Robinson goes on to show the point at issue. His view of church and state was entirely different from that of Bishop Hall. It related to "the nearness of the state and church. We indeed have much wickedness in the city where we live, you in the church, but in earnest, do you imagine we account the kingdom of England 'Babylon'? or the city of Amsterdam 'Zion'? It is the Church of England or state ecclesiastical, which we account Babylon, and from which we withdraw in spiritual communion. But for the commonwealth or kingdom as we honour it above all the states in the world, so would we thankfully embrace the meanest corner in it, at the extremest conditions of any people in the kingdom. The hellish impieties in the city of Amsterdam do no more prejudice our heavenly communion in the church of Christ, than the frogs, lice, murrain, and other plagues overspreading Egypt, did the Israelites when Goshen, the portion of their inheritance, was free." What Robinson objected to was the failure to make the proper distinction between Church and State. To him, the Church was gathered *out* of the community, it was *not* everyone who resided in the Parish. The issue of Church and State, while not completely worked out in New England, was at the heart of the principles worked out by Robinson and the "Independents" who followed him. It is still a vital issue in the U.S.A., and is relevant in this country, too.

Robinson was a Congregationalist, and his influence can be seen in the principles of the first Church of Christ in New England, as drawn up by Mr. Prince in his New England Chronology. They are the following:

1. That no particular church ought to consist of more members than can conveniently watch over one another, and usually meet and worship in one congregation.
2. That every particular Church of Christ is only to consist of such as appear to believe in and obey Him.
3. That any competent number of such, when their consciences oblige them, have a right to embody into a church for their mutual edification.
4. That this embodying is by some certain contract or covenant, either expressed or implied, though it ought to be by the former.
5. That being embodied, they have a right of choosing all their officers.
6. That the officers appointed by Christ for this embodied church are, in some respects, of three sorts, in others but two, namely

(i) Pastors, or teaching Elders, who have the power both of overseeing, teaching, administering the sacraments, and ruling too, and being chiefly to give themselves to studying, teaching, and the spiritual care of the flock, are therefore to be maintained.

Mere ruling Elders, who are to help the Pastors in overseeing and ruling; that their offices be not temporary, as among the Dutch and French churches, but continual; and being also qualified in some degree to teach, they are to teach only occasionally, through necessity, or in their Pastor's absence or illness; but being not to give themselves to study or teaching, they have no need of maintenance.

That the Elders of both sorts form the Presbytery of overseers and rulers, which should be in every particular church; and are in Scripture called sometimes Presbyters, or Elders, sometimes Bishops or Overseers, and sometimes Rulers.

(ii) Deacons, who are to take care of the poor, and of the church's treasure; to distribute for the support of the Pastor, the supply of the needy, the propagation of religion, and to minister at the Lord's Table, etc.

(iii) That these officers, being chosen and ordained, have no lordly, arbitrary, or imposing power but can only rule and minister with the consent of the brethren.

(iv) That no churches, or church officer whatever, have any power over any church or officers, to control or impose upon them; but are equal in their rights and privileges, and ought to be independent in the exercise and enjoyment of them.

(v) As to Church administrations, they held that Baptism is a seal of the covenants of grace, and hold be dispensed only to visible believers with their unadult children; and this in primitive purity, as in the times of Christ and His Apostles, without the sign of the cross, or any other invented ceremony. And that the church or its officers have no authority to inflict any penalties of a temporal nature, excommunication being wholly spiritual in a rejection of the scandalous from the communion of the church.

(vi) And lastly, as for Holy Days; they were very strict for the observation of the Lord's Day, in a pious memory of the Incarnation, Birth, Death, Resurrection, Ascension, and Benefits of Christ; as also solemn Fastings and Thanksgivings as the state of Providence requires. But all other times not prescribed in Scripture they utterly relinquished. And as in general they could not conceive anything a part of Christ's religion, which he has not required, they therefore renounced all human right of inventing, and much less of imposing it on others.

It is evident from the foregoing that, in theory, he believed that the congregation could overthrow the government of the church quite simply, by a majority vote. In practice, however, the congregation at Leyden gave him and Brewster great respect, and Robinson urged them to submit to Brewster in his absence. He also spoke otherwise on the subject. "Wise men," he says, "having written of this subject, have approved as good and lawful, three kinds of polities, monarchical, where supreme authority is in the hands of one; aristocratical, when it is in the hands of some few select persons; and democratical, in the whole body or multitude. And all these three forms have their places in the church of Christ. In respect of Him, the Head, it is a monarchy, in respect of the eldership, an aristocracy; in respect of the body, a popular state."

However, there was a dispute between himself and the Amsterdam church on the authority of the Elders, the latter giving them power to rule and not merely to act as executives. Trying experiences taught them the need of this. Robinson could well maintain his authority in a congregational system, such was his calibre, but many New England pastors had great difficulties. It was said that in England the clergy dominated the people, but in New England the congregation dominated the ministers! The Amsterdam church became Baptist, but Robinson held to infant Baptism.

It is important to recognise a theological distinction among the early Separatists. John Robinson, before 1610, was much of one mind with the other Separatists, but after he met Henry Jacob, the founder of the first Congregational Church, became more an Independent than a Separatist in his attitude towards the Church of England. His treatise on "The Lawfulness of Hearing Ministers in the Church of England" demonstrates that he was censured by some who held an extreme view of the spiritual condition of the Church of England. John Robinson, along with most of those who came to be called "Independents", did not regard the Church of England as being entirely false, but recognised that there were many within that body who were true Ministers of God, and many congregations that were true churches. His contact with the Puritans that were in the Establishment, particularly those at Cambridge, would have convinced him of the reality of their faith.

We are not to imagine they gave great stress to external matters, as did the late Victorian Evangelicals. It may come as a surprise to some that they were fond of beer and only wore black and grey clothes on Sabbath days. Unlike their Puritan neighbours at Boston they passed no laws against gay apparel, but wore bright clothes during the week. Ruling Elder, William Brewster, had a red cap, a white cap, a quilted cap, a laced cap, a violet coat and "one pair of green draws"!

Having thus considered the principles of John Robinson and the Pilgrim Fathers, we should ask ourselves the question, "What is the point of looking into this whole historical episode? Is it simply of interest to antiquarians?" Some see the issues they fought for as dead and gone. We live in a different world and religious persecution is rare. Having had in my study for the past twelve years the picture of the sailing of the *Mayflower* from Southampton, and a number of books on the subject, I have been impressed by the tremendous contrast the Pilgrims present to the life of the churches today. Of course, it is 350 years later, but have they nothing to teach us? There was a depth of conviction which made them willing to be rejected by the religious world. We are surrounded by superficial thinking. The greatest heresy, it seems, is to take the things of God too seriously, and to find onself at odds with the thinking of the majority. There was a spiritual unity and family feeling that can scarcely be discovered anywhere outside the New Testament. We hear a great deal about Church Unity these days. It is *the great* issue. Have we forgotten that when the unity of the people of God is spoken of in Scripture it generally relates to the local congregation? What is more costly in human and spiritual terms than to live in peace and harmony in a company of people drawn from all sections of the community? What is more impressive in a world that is growing harder and more selfish all the time than a group of people who only have in common *spiritual* interests, yet who love and care for one another! What is needed in these days is not larger ecclesiastical units, but local congregations that practise what they preach. Truly, the Pilgrims were the salt of the earth, and their principles were a light that has powerfully influenced what has become the greatest nation in the history of mankind.

What was it that made John Robinson such a remarkable man? His understanding of the basic doctrines of the faith were identical with those of the Protestant Anglican Reformers, as expressed in the 39 Articles, and the Presbyterians, in the Westminster Confession. In short, he was an orthodox "Calvinist". His famous statement that "God has yet more truth and light to break forth out of His Holy Word", must not be construed as the sentiments of a free-thinker, since he limited Redemptive Revelation to "His Holy Word". His essay on the Scriptures, in Chapter 6, makes this clear. It was his *submission to God through His Word, by faith*, that led him to act as he did. The world was hostile then to that which he found in the Scriptures, and it always will be. His ambition, as a wise pastor, did not only extend as far as this life, in the continuance of a Testimony to biblical Christianity, but beyond. He looked for the day when, like Paul concerning the Corinthians, he would "present" his people "as a chaste virgin to Christ", 2 Cor. 11. 2. He might well have said concerning them, as Paul did concerning the Thessalonians, "What is our hope, or joy, or crown of rejoicing? Are not even ye in the presence of our Lord Jesus Christ at his coming? For ye are our glory and joy," 1 Thess. 2. 19, 20. No lesser ambition would do for one whose sole authority was the Word of God, nor could any lesser goal account for the remarkable success he had. The essays in Chapter 6 have been chosen to show both his orthodoxy and his pastoral skill. It might be well that there should be an absence of "Envy", "Slander", "Flattery" and "Suspicion" among the flock for the good of all, not least the pastor! But for the glory of Christ, the great Head of the Church Himself was preparing His people for the day when He would present them to Himself, with all God's people from every part and every age, "a glorious church, not having spot, or wrinkle, or any such thing; but that it should be holy and without blemish" (Eph. 5. 27).

CHAPTER SIX

We listen to Pastor Robinson

THE FOLLOWING have been selected and abbreviated from John Robinson's Essays. They do not make easy reading, since they were written in a day when the art of "communication" was largely ignored. However, those who take the trouble to read them carefully will be richly rewarded. Cold print cannot possibly convey the grace and power of Robinson's words, but they may reflect a little of his wisdom and knowledge of things Divine. We have witnessed over the past twenty years a remarkable interest in the spiritual heritage that exists in this country. However, it has not touched the corporate life of the local church to any marked degree. There is no substitute for a local congregation in which the grace of God is corporately manifested. Robinson's constant care, in his ministry and practical pastoral work, was the Divine instrument used. The last four essays bring us close to the heart of the Christian's warfare, and the enemies within that must be dealt with. Was it not because the Pilgrims had dealt first with the enemies within that they could tackle adversaries and adversities outside of themselves?

OF THE HOLY SCRIPTURES

The holy Scriptures are that Divine instrument by which we are taught what to believe, concerning God ourselves, and all things, and how to please God unto eternal life.

God has had His will written in the Scriptures for more certainty of truth to men, and to preserve it the better from being corrupted; also for the unity of churches and Christians in the same truth; and also, for general use; seeing books and writings may both easily be dispersed whither the voice of teachers cannot come.

I. THE SCRIPTURES—GOD'S REVELATION

Not everything wherein the prophets of God wrote wherein they were divinely inspired was made part of the canonical Scriptures, which we call the Bible; no more than all which they spake by the Spirit was written, John xx. 30; xxi. 25: but only so much, as the Lord in wisdom, and mercy, thought requisite to guide the church in faith and obedience, to the world's end; so as the Scriptures should neither be defective through brevity, nor burdensome by too great largeness. Here we may observe God's providence in preserving the Scriptures from miscarrying; and the Church's care, and faithfulness in keeping safe this heavenly treasure.

The Scriptures are not only authentic in themselves, as having the Spirit of God for the author both of matter, and manner, and writing, 2 Pet. i. 21; but do also, as they say, carry their authority in their mouths, binding both to faith and obedience, all whomsoever, unto whom they come, and by what means soever. And if God "left not himself without witness", Acts xiv. 17, in His works of creation, and providence; how much less in his written Word? wherein, without comparison, He reveals himself much more clearly, than the other way: which is therefore discernible by itself. Their assertion, therefore, who hold, and teach, that we are to receive the Scriptures for the churches' testimony, is in effect none other, than that we are to believe God for men's cause: whereas, on the contrary, if a man should find the book of the Holy Scriptures in the highway, or hidden under a stone, yet he were bound to learn, receive, believe, and obey them, and every part of them. And if the word preached by Christ, the prophets, and apostles, in their time, whether to Jews, or Gentiles, were absolutely to be believed, and obeyed, by everyone that heard it, without further testimony; why not as well, and much, now by all that read it written?

II. THE PERFECTION OF SCRIPTURE

The profit and power of the Scriptures, both for stay of faith, and rule of life, and comfort in all manner of afflictions, no tongue or pen is able so fully to express, as every true Christian finds, and feels, in his own experience. There is but one true happiness, life eternal: one giver of it, God; one Mediator, Jesus Christ; and so but one means of imparting it, the word of God: by which, he that is both author and finisher of all, both begins, and perfects all. "Blessed is the man, that hath his delight therein, and meditates in the same, day and night" Psa. i. 1, 2: that so he may learn the things upon earth, the knowledge whereof will fit him for heaven.

When we avow the Scriptures' perfection, we exclude not from men common sense, and the light of nature. Yea, besides other human helps, we both acknowledge, and beg of God as most needful for their fruitful understanding, the light of his Holy Spirit: only we avow them as a most perfect rule neither crooked any way, nor short in anything requisite. This their sufficiency and perfection is not to be restrained to matters simply necessary to salvation. But to matters necessary to obedience, that we may please God in all things, great or small. "Without faith we cannot please God," Heb. xi. 6; and "Faith comes only by the word of God", Rom. x. 17; which we must therefore make our guide in "all our ways". Prov. iii. 6. And if we be to "give an account of every idle word" Matt. xii. 36, and so for every vain thought, or work, there is then a law of God for these smallest matters; for where no law is, there is no transgression, and where there is no transgression, or fault, there is no account to be given. And if the holy Scriptures' direction reach unto the whole course of our life, how much more of our religion, or worship of God? in which nothing is to be practised, but that which is to be believed; nothing to be believed, but that which is to be taught; nothing to be taught, but according to the Scriptures. This being the first thing that we are to believe, that we must believe nothing, but according to them. All things else are human; and human it is to err, and be deceived.

III. THE TRANSLATION OF SCRIPTURE

As the title set over the head of Christ crucified, was the same in Hebrew, Greek, and Latin, so are the Scriptures the same, whether in the original, or other language into which they are faithfully translated. Yet, as the waters are most pure, and sweet in the fountain, so are all writings, Divine and human, in their original tongues; it being impossible, but some either change, or defect, or redundancy will be found in the translation, either by default of the translator, or of the tongue, into which it is made.

In a translator is required, specially, skill in words, and tongues; in an expositor, judgment in things. That translation is most exact, which agreeth best with the original, word for word, so far as the idiom, or propriety of the language will bear.

IV. THE INTERPRETATION OF SCRIPTURE

As the law-maker best knows the meaning of the law, and how it is to be expounded, so for the exposition of the holy Scriptures, the Spirit of God, as the author thereof is first and most to be consulted with, by faithful and earnest prayer, from a good conscience, that God may fulfil his promise made of "giving his Holy Spirit to them that ask it", Luke xi. 13, and of "revealing his secrets to them that fear him", Psa. xxv. 14. And so some special instruments of renewing the gospel's light in the former age, have professed, that they learned more this way by prayer, than by much study otherwise.

Rules of Interpretation

There is in Scripture but one proper, and immediate sense; others are rather collections from it, relations unto it, or illustrations of it, than immediate senses. The literal sense is to be followed, as being most natural what may be, and not to be refused, if it may stand without danger, and according to other

Scriptures. And here it must be noted, that Christ, and his apostles in expounding Moses and the prophets, did not only infallibly express their conceptions and meanings, but the meaning of the Spirit speaking in them; and that, by reason of their more plentiful measure of the same Spirit and experience withal, in some particulars, as I conceive, further than the prophets themselves understood. All God's laws and instructions must, in honour of lawgiver, be expounded in the largest sense that they can bear: that so they may reach as far, and bind as fast, as may be. And as they are blame-worthy, who out of a scrupulous fear, lest they should add to the Scriptures, allow them no further meaning, than the words express; so is their sin greater, and full of presumption, who shorten and straiten the Scriptures' instruction to that which is expressed in so many words, that they may make room thereby, for their own devices. A scripture commandeth, promiseth, or threateneth whatsoever is contained in it, which can truly and justly be gathered from it.

Particular words and phrases, more obscure, are to be interpreted according to the scope and mind of the speaker, the Holy Ghost. Neither is the scripture profitable except the scope be first found. And to hang upon a word, phrase, or sentence in a text, without looking to the main drift, is, if any other, the character of an heretical disposition. With this, that other most necessary rule hath affinity; namely, that the words are to be understood according to the subject matter.

As we oft find out, and learn men's meaning by some of their company, and of such as are about them, which we could not learn of themselves, so may we gather the meaning of a scripture, otherwise hard to be understood, by marking the things which accompany it, and which are above and below, as the Jews used to speak, and Christians with them.

Like as the lamps in the golden candlestick did one help another's light; so doth one place of holy scripture, another's. And though a thing found in one place to insist upon it, in a difference, as to neglect others, is the highway to error, and to lose the right sense, by breaking the scripture's golden chain, whose links are all fastened together. And as one place must be expounded by another; so must the more brief and obscure by the more plain and large, and not the contrary, and cross way: for that were not to lighten the darkness of a text, but to darken its light: according as it has been said "The fewer must be understood according to the more, and one saying must rather be taken accordingly to all, than against all".

V. THE USE OF HELPS

Lastly, he that will expound the Scriptures, with respect to the graces of God bestowed upon other men, and in regard to his own infirmity should make use of the commentaries and expositions of such special instruments, as God in mercy hath raised up for the opening of them, and edifying the church thereby: remembering always, that "the word of God neither came from him nor to him alone" 1 Cor. xiv. 36. He that depends too much upon other men's judgment, makes as if the word of God came not to himself at all: he that neglects it, as if it came to him only.

It is strange, and lamentable, that, in the great profession of the Scriptures made in our days, so many should be ignorant of the difference between the law, and the gospel, of which two heads the Scriptures consist: making the gospel nothing else, but a more favourable, and easy law; a promise to be received, into a commandment to be fulfilled: and the offering of a new life, even the life of Christ, into the exacting of old, and due debt only. Gal. ii. 20.

VI. ONLY ONE GOSPEL GIVEN

The utmost ordinary means of revelation of God's will for man's salvation and happiness, is the gospel. When the law written in man's heart by creation was almost worn out, God gave it written in tables of stone. But life, and freedom from sin, and death, being "impossible to the law in that it was weak, through the flesh", Rom. viii. 3; and all men by it, whether considered as written in tablets of stone, or of the heart, by creation, "coming short of the glory of God", Rom. iii. 23; it hath pleased the same God by the gospel of his Son Christ to provide a gracious remedy, that the sick to death, by the justice of the law might be cured; yea the dead revived, by the grace of the gospel, and mercy of God therein. And other remedy besides, and beyond this, for the obtaining of salvation, God hath not revealed. He that fulfils not the righteousness of the law, violates God's justice: but remaining obstinate against the grace of the gospel also, he despises, with God's justice, his mercy; and his authority in both. And what remains for such, but a fearful expectation of the work of his terrible power, of "the revelation of his wrath from heaven against all, specially such, ungodliness of men"? Rom. i. 8. "For if the word [of the law] spoken by angels was stedfast, and every transgression and disobedience received a just recompense of reward; how shall we escape, if we neglect so great a salvation [of the gospel]; which at first, began to be preached by the Lord, and was confirmed to us by them that heard him"? Heb. ii. 2, 3.

OF GOD'S LOVE

God loveth himself first and most as the chiefest good, and all other good things as he communicates with them the effects of his own goodness. And from this infinite love he severely punisheth some creatures, through the work of his own hands. For, first, the creature by sin violates God's holiness, and despises his authority in his righteous commandments in hardness of heart and unbelief; and since it is impossible, that God's love of his own holiness, and justice, and the love of the creature's happiness, who so obstinately dishonours him, should stand together; it must be that the latter must give way to the former, and the creature must become miserable, rather than God disregard his own honour and glory.

God reveals his glorious Majesty in the highest heavens, his fearful justice in the hell of the damned; his wise and powerful providence is manifest throughout the whole world; but his gracious love and mercy in, and unto his church here upon earth; which he therefore hath chosen, and taken near unto himself, that in it might be seen the riches of his glorious grace. And though all things in God are infinite, and one, yet are the effects of his love more wonderful, and excellent, than of any other of his attributes; as appears in his greatest work of giving his only begotten Son to the cursed death of the cross for his enemies out of his love and mercy. This the Scriptures, and worthily, call a "great mystery", 1 Tim. iii. 16, and which, for the rareness of it, was not only "hidden from the sons of men", Eph. iii. 5 but also from the very angels in their perfection of created knowledge. Which manifold grace, and wisdom of God they, therefore, "desire to look into, and learn by the church", 1 Pet. i. 10–12.

Love in the creature ever presupposeth some good, true or apparent in the thing loved, by which that affection of union is drawn. But the love of God on the contrary, causeth all good to be produced in the creature. He first loveth us in the free purpose of his will, and thence worketh good for us and in us. And hence come the unchangeableness of God's love towards us, because it is founded in himself, and in the stableness of the good pleasure of his own will. And although we may be comforted as we observe our love to him; yet is far greater comfort drawn from the consideration of His love to us; as being not only the ground of the other, but in him also infinite, and unchangeable. And, hereupon, it was that the sisters of Lazarus seeking help for their sick brother sent Christ word, not that he, who loved him, but that "he whom he loved, was sick", John xi. 3.

As by the hand of a friend reached unto us we are made partakers of the strength of his whole body to hold us up, so by the hand of the love of God reached down from heaven in the Gospel we become aware of all His other attributes. The more wise, powerful, holy, glorious, eternal, and infinite God is, the more happy are we because of his love, and mercy in Christ, which moveth Him to use them all for our good, and to communicate them with us, as his friends, so far as serves for our happiness. He, whom God loves though he know it not, is a happy man: he that knows it, knows himself to be happy. From this "love of God", as from a spring-head comes all good both for grace, and glory. Yea by it, which is more, all evil by all creatures intended, or done against us, is turned good to us. By it our afflictions work together with our election, redemption, vocation, etc., for our good. By reason of it "the stones of the field are at league with us, and the beasts of the field at peace with us", Job. v. 23: yea even the very sword that killeth us, the fire that burneth us, and the water that drowneth us, is a kind of spiritual, and invisible league with us, to do us good. Upon the knowledge of this "love of God shed abroad into our hearts by the Holy Ghost", is laid the foundation, and ground-work of whatsoever good thing we return again unto God. Upon this we do build our faith, and confidence in him, by this our cold and frozen hearts are not only thawed, but inflamed also with love again to him, and to men for him: as the earth being heated by the beams of the sun beating upon it, reflecteth heat again towards the heavens, and upon all the bodies between it, and them. Lastly, from hence arise all the pleasing services, wherewith we present His Majesty. We can do nothing as we ought, but from the faith, and feeling of His love in Christ. But being once drawn sweetly by the cords of God's goodness, and love, we readily follow after him; as being debtors and constrained, not by necessity, but by love.

The tokens of this "love of God" in Christ are not only by us highly to be prized, but carefully to be discerned; lest we bring ourselves into a fool's paradise, and grow presumptuously secure; which is the forerunner of sudden, and certain destruction. We must therefore in this scrutiny neither trust ourselves, nor any other creature, but God alone in the testimony of his

Word, and the Spirit, which "knows, and makes known the mind of God", 1 Cor. ii. 10–12; and by which we may unerringly learn; *first*, what the tokens of his love are; and *secondly*, who they are which partake of them; and *thirdly*, that we ourselves are of that blessed number. Now, amongst them all, there is none so certain, and infallible as the gracious work of true repentance in the "mortifying of the old man in his sinful affections", Rom. viii. 13. As we may certainly know, that the sun shines, by the beams, and heat thereof below, though we climb not into heaven to see, so may we have certain knowledge of God's gracious love towards us, without searching further than our own hearts, and ways, and by finding them truly, and effectually turned from sin to God.

OF GOD'S PROMISES

God ever performeth what He promiseth, and not one good thing for another, as some think.

OF ENVY

Envy is a grief conceived at the good of another;[1] specially, by him that wants it himself:[2] whereof the highest degree is, so to envy it to him, as we desire it ourselves. It is a very shameful affection, and which no man will own, how many soever use it. Some will confess and profess, upon occasion, that they hate, or fear, or scorn others; but none that they envy any.[3] And no marvel; for though many deserve to be hated, feared and despised, yet none, to be envied.

He that envieth maketh another man's virtue, his vice, as Bernard confesseth of himself,[4] and another man's happiness, his torment:[5] whereas, he that rejoiceth at the prosperity of another, is partaker of the same. It is horrible impiety, to complain of

[1] Plutarch.   [2] Cyprian.   [3] Plutarch.
[4] Bernard.   [5] Politian.

God, that he made the world no better: but what is it than to quarrel with him for making it so good: as in truth, an envious person doth, saying unto God, in effect, Why hast thou bestowed this virtue, this knowledge, this honour, these riches, or the like good upon this man, or woman? So the "first labourers in the vineyard said of the last, to him which hired them; Why givest thou so much unto them?" Matt. xx, 10–12. How injurious this cankerworm is both to God and men.

The good gifts of God, as riches, honour, wit, learning, etc., in any eminency often endanger their owners by puffing them up with pride in themselves: and if they have the grace, and modesty to use them aright yet are they dangerous to others, becoming often fuel to kindle their fire of envy withal. And so it fell out between Joseph and his brethren, David and king Saul, and many more; verifying that of the wise man—"Every perfection of work is the envy of a man from his neighbour." Eccl. iv. 4. By means whereof it also hurts its owner, many times, by a kind of unnatural rebound, as it were from the envious. And in this regard, a mediocrity in any good is the more thankfully to be accepted from God; considering unto what danger this way, all eminency exposeth a man. The highest trees are soonest and sorest shaken with tempests.

The best remedy for preventing envy by others, is to carry a low sail in the most prosperous gale that can blow: and to ascribe the good a man hath rather to any other cause, than to himself, or his own wit, industry, or worth any way. Therein he least disparageth others that want it, and so frees himself best from their envy at him.

OF SLANDER

He is a slanderer, who wrongs his neighbour's credit, either by unjust raising or upholding an evil report against him.[1] Of which two, viz., the raising, or receiving a false report, seeing that i

[1] Bernard.

there were no receivers, there would be no thieves, one of good skill in discerning, doubteth whether is more damnable. We must then get amongst others, this mark of him that shall sojourn in the Lord's tabernacle, and dwell in his holy mountain, that we neither raise, nor take, or hold up a reproach against our neighbour. Ps. xv. 1-5. Though the north wind be not always to be wished, because it driveth away rain, yet is an "angry countenance to drive away a backbiting tongue." Prov. xxv. 23.

Sometimes men without just and necessary occasion blaze abroad the faults of others; either in idleness, for want of other talk; or of hatred, by way of revenge; or in flattery, to please other men; or in envy, as grudging at their good name. And it may well be thought, that persons oftener slander others of love to themselves, than of hatred to them; thinking therein to build their own credit, upon the ruins of other men's; which is, as if one to make his own garment seem the fairer, should cast mire upon his neighbour's.

Slanderers may be called devilish, seeing the devil hath his name of slandering. He sometimes slanders God to men; as to Eve, of envy, in the beginning, Gen. iii. 1-6: sometimes men to God; as Job of hypocrisy, Job. i. 9-12; and, continually, man to man.

David never complains of the sharpness of the swords of the Philistines, or other enemies; but of the sharp swords of the tongue of slanderers, he oft, and piteously complains in the book of Psalms, as piercing deeper than the former. Ps. 3, 57, 58, 64, etc. And yet, for fence against those sharp swords, God hath put into the hands of his innocent servants two bucklers; and one inward, viz. a conscience, upon due knowledge; and examination excusing before God: the other, such a conversation before men, as may ward our credit and good name from being wounded in the eyes of such as know us. Yet, if the devil could by the serpent's slanders impeach the credit of God himself with our first parents, in their state of innocency, no marvel, if his serpentlike instruments can prevail with sinful men and women this way, even against God's faithful servants. We must therefore prevent slanders when we can; bear what we cannot avoid; and always be mindful by earnest prayer, as well to commend our good name to God, that he may take charge of it, as our persons and estates.

Better never accused, than quit, though after the clearest, and most honourable manner, that may be; seeing after a bold slander something ever will stick behind. But how great soever matter of grief or shame unjust slander causeth; yet he that is "reproached for well-doing, hath the spirit of glory resting upon him," 1 Pet. iv. 14.

OF FLATTERY

A man needs no other flatterer than his own partial heart to infatuate him. Notwithstanding, though few would rather buy a false, than a true glass to see their faces in, yet how few are there so truly hating their own vices, as that they had not rather seek, or at least, entertain such friends, as may rather cover their faults by flatteries, than cure them by faithful reproofs. And this benefit, men of a poor and despised condition may set against divers miseries incident thereunto, that they are thereby out of danger of being much flattered. Every one will be bold to call a poor man, fool, or knave, and to speak of and to him all the ill which he knows, and more also. Whereas the rich and mighty in the world are, for the most part, soothed up to their destruction; as the fat ox is stroked by the same hand that strikes him down. And this is just from God upon the most of them, because they desire rather to be pleased by flatteries, than bettered by hearing the truth. Few coming near David's order, will say as he did, "Let the righteous smite me, it shall be a kindness: let him reprove me, it shall be a precious oil." Psalm cxli. 5.

Flattery is in all cases and persons a base sin, and which will make one man, dog-like, to fawn upon another, for a morsel of bread, Prov. xxviii. 21. But in the ministers of God's holy

Word, above all other men, is most pernicious. This made the apostle "take God to witness, that he never used flattering words", 1 Thess. ii. 5; and to protest against others, that they in doing it, "served not the Lord Jesus, but their own bellies." Rom. xvi. 18.

OF SUSPICION

Suspicion, as it is commonly taken, is as it were, looking under a hidden thing, with an inclination to judge it evil and amiss. It sets the person suspected in a kind of middle state, but something bended the worse way, and neither quit because he is suspected; nor condemned, because he is but suspected.[1]

Some suspect all men, and some none: both are in fault; the former in the most sinful fault, the latter in the most honest, but more dangerous to themselves. And yet, even for that, there want not, who by causeless suspicion teach their servants, friends, yea wives, and children also, to deceive them.[2] For many respecting more their credit with men, than a good conscience before God, by being suspected, though causelessly, grow desperate. It is best therefore, first not to suspect without good cause; next, not to betray our suspicion, except we have great hope to overawe thereby the suspected person.

There are many, transported from the one of the extremes formerly mentioned to the other: who being at first credulous, and light of belief, and thereby oft deceived, at length come to trust none; but would burn, as they say, their shirt, if they thought it knew their secrets: and therefore set it down for a rule, to have all men in jealousy. Howsoever things fall out, it is best to keep our bias always on the right side; and to incline still to a better, rather than to a worse opinion of men, than they deserve. For though it be best of all, to judge of others just as they are: yet seeing that is always hard and sometimes impossible, we shall less offend God in judging of men too well, though

[1] Suetonius.　　　　[2] Seneca.

sometimes to our own damage, than too ill, with certain injury to them, and sin in ourselves, in the violation of the law of charity, which "is not suspicious". 1 Cor. xiii. 5.

The general cause of suspicion is the want of this true love, whose property is to believe all things and to hope all things, which with reason can be believed or hoped for.

He that is good himself, doth not easily suspect another to be evil: nor the evil, that another is good. [1] Besides, an evil conscience accusing men and women, that they in truth deserve not love, nor respect, nor credit, easily persuades them, that they are not loved, nor respected, nor credited by others. Lastly, it is often a punishment from God, that as a man in debt, suspects that every bush which he sees, is a serjeant to arrest him; so they which are without true grace, and assurance of the pardon of their sins from him, should be suspicious, that every one would deceive, or hurt them otherwise. It was God's curse upon Cain, when he had killed his brother Abel, to suspect and fear that everyone that he met with, would kill him. Gen. iv. 14. We must always strive for that discretion and wisdom, as not to take our marks amiss, by censuring any rashly, as Eli did Hannah for drunkenness, because her lips went, and her voice was not heard: nor yet to be so fondly charitable, as not to see the spots of men's leprosy breaking out in their foreheads.

We are not only by innocency to prevent just blame; but withal, by Christian care, and wisdom, to provide that we hurt not our good name by coming under suspicion of evil. We provide things honest before God by preserving innocency; but before men, by giving no probable cause of their suspecting us. And so doing, if yet God by his providence, so ordered, that we come under it; we must bear it patiently, as a burden laid upon us by him, either to prove us; as it was not the least trial upon Job.

[1] Chrysostom.